COMMUNICATION

Project Consultant

Harriet Diamond
Diamond Associates
Westfield, NJ

Series Reviewers

Nancy Arnold
Metropolitan Adult
Education Program
San Jose, CA

Lou Winn Burns
Booker High School
Sarasota, FL

Jane Westbrook
Weatherford ISD
Community Services
Weatherford, TX

Ronald D. Froman
National Training &
Development Specialists
Winter Springs, FL

Dr. Randy Whitfield
North Carolina Community
College System
Raleigh, NC

STECK-VAUGHN
C O M P A N Y
ELEMENTARY • SECONDARY • ADULT • LIBRARY

Acknowledgments

Steck-Vaughn Company
Executive Editor: Ellen Northcutt
Supervising Editor: Tim Collins
Senior Editor: Julie Higgins
Assistant Art Director: Richard Balsam
Design Manager: Danielle Szabo

Proof Positive/Farrowlyne Associates, Inc.
Program Editorial, Development, Design, and Production

Photo Credits
Cover Photo: © John Levy/Gamma-Liaison
Pp. 4, 6, 7, 12, 14, 15, 20, 21, 22, 28, 29, 31, 37, 38, 46, 47, 52, 53, 54, 62, 63, 69, 70, 77, 78 © From: The ENTER HERE® Series, © 1995 by Enter Here L.L.C.; p. 36 © Walter Hodges/Tony Stone Images; p. 44 © Chip Henderson/Index Stock Photography; p. 60 © Bruce Ayres/Tony Stone Images; p. 68 © Jon Riley/Tony Stone Images; p. 76 © Stewart Cohen/Index Stock Photography.

ISBN 0–8172–6517–1

2 3 4 5 6 7 8 9 DBH 01 00 99 98 97

Contents

To the Learner

Workforce: Building Success is a series of six books designed to help you improve key job skills. You will find many ways to improve your skills, whether you're already working or you're preparing to find a job. This book, *Communication,* is about ways to speak and listen better at work. To succeed at work, you need to talk to and understand coworkers, customers, and bosses.

Before you begin the lessons, take the Check What You Know skills inventory, check your own answers, and fill out the Preview Chart. There you will see which skills you already know and which you need to practice.

After you finish the last practice page, take the Check What You've Learned inventory, check your answers, and fill out the Review Chart. You'll see what great progress you've made.

Each lesson is followed by four types of exercises:

- The questions in **Comprehension Check** will help you make sure you understood the reading.
- In **Making Connections,** you will read about situations in which people need to use the skills in the reading.
- In the next section, called **Try It Out, Act It Out,** or **Talk It Out,** you will complete an activity that requires you to use the new skills. You might interview someone, conduct a survey, make a telephone call, have a discussion, or act out a situation.
- In **Think and Apply,** you will think about how well you use the skills in your daily life. Then you will decide which skills you want to improve and make a plan to reach your goal.

At the end of the book, you will find a Glossary and an Answer Key. Use the glossary to look up definitions of key work-related words. Use the Answer Key to check your answers to many of the exercises.

Check What You Know

Check What You Know will help you know how well you understand communication skills. It will also show you which skills you need to improve.

Read each question. Circle the letter before the answer.

1. Julie is the manager of a software store. She gets a call from an angry customer. He has been waiting three weeks for a special order. Julie should

   a. apologize and tell him she'll have an answer later that day.
   b. complain about the software store.
   c. say that she doesn't know.

2. Liza works as a word processor. On Friday she finishes her work early, at three o'clock. Then she sees that Dan, another word processor on her team, needs to finish two large documents. Liza should

   a. go home early and enjoy the weekend.
   b. ask Dan if she can help him finish his typing.
   c. tell Dan he needs to get on the ball and start typing faster.

3. Mindy asked Sarah to type a report. When Sarah gives the report to Mindy, Mindy notices several serious mistakes in the report. Sarah is a new secretary and not completely familiar with the computer program. Mindy should

   a. give the next report to someone else to do.
   b. politely point out the mistakes and suggest Sarah get additional computer training.
   c. tell all of Sarah's coworkers that she's incompetent.

4. Sam works in a cafeteria. He was just put in charge of soups. Gloria, Sam's boss, shows him how to make soup. As she is showing him, Sam should

   a. suggest someone else make the soups.
   b. be silent so Gloria will think he understands perfectly.
   c. ask questions if he is unsure of something.

5. Tim asked Nancy to type a report. Nancy did an excellent job, and she corrected two spelling mistakes that Tim made in the report. Tim should tell Nancy,

a. "You did a good job on that report."
b. "Your work on that report wasn't that bad at all."
c. "Please do not correct my spelling mistakes any more."

6. Terrence is a telephone operator for a mail-order company. He gets a call from a customer who is difficult to understand. Terrence should

a. repeat what the customer said and ask if that's correct.
b. angrily tell the customer he can't understand.
c. hang up.

7. Daria is a checkout clerk in a grocery store. She'd like to take Thursday off. Another clerk, Josh, works on Saturdays but wants this Saturday off. Daria usually does not work on weekends. Daria does not like to work on Saturdays, but no one else can trade shifts with her. Daria should

a. call in sick on Thursday.
b. compromise and ask Josh to trade shifts this week.
c. not show up for work on Thursday.

8. Marta has just been promoted to assistant manager of a clothing store. She wants to share her ideas on how to display the sportswear at tomorrow's meeting. At the meeting, Marta should

a. tell everyone about her ideas and insist on using them.
b. keep quiet and tell the manager her ideas after the meeting.
c. tell the others about her ideas and listen to their ideas, too.

9. Gilbert is a ticket agent with an airline. He is attending a class to learn the airline's new ticketing system. Gilbert's car broke down this morning, and he is finding it difficult to concentrate. He should

   a. listen carefully and focus on the training class.

   b. think about his car and how expensive the repairs will be.

   c. leave class early and call the garage to see if his car is ready.

10. Eric works as a library assistant. Eric's supervisor tells Eric she is unhappy with his work. Eric should

    a. get defensive and shout that his supervisor is wrong.

    b. walk out of the meeting.

    c. ask his supervisor what is expected of him.

Preview Chart

This chart will show you what skills you need to study. Reread each question you missed. Then look at the appropriate lesson of the book for help in understanding the correct answer.

Question Check the questions you missed.	Skill The exercise, like the book, focuses on the skills below.	Lesson Preview what you will learn in this book.
1. _____	Handling business calls	10
2. _____	Being a team player	8
3. _____	Giving helpful feedback	7
4. _____	Getting information	2
5. _____	Giving a positive message	4
6. _____	Giving directions	3
7. _____	Reaching a compromise	6
8. _____	Working with others	5
9. _____	Listening	1
10. _____	Communicating with your boss	9

Listening Effectively

How can you tell someone is listening to you?

How do you show others you are listening to them?

Listening carefully can help you build positive work relationships.

Whether you are talking with clients, customers, coworkers, or supervisors, it is important to listen and to show you are listening. In a large manufacturing plant, you might nod in agreement rather than say "yes" over noise. If you work in an office, you might need to listen to understand specific details of your supervisor's instructions. Sometimes you listen to learn the main idea of the speaker's message. Other times you listen to respond to the speaker. Listening is a skill that you can always improve. This lesson will present seven ways you can improve your listening skills.

Focus

How do you gather as much information as possible from your speaker? Let your speaker know that he or she is the center of your attention. Shut out the rest of the world while you listen. It may be hard not to drift away. But if you don't focus, you may miss something. Remind yourself to pay attention. Try not to think about other matters. One way to focus is to pretend that the speaker's words travel through a tunnel from the speaker to you. Don't let anything else get in the way.

Make Eye Contact

You should look straight at the person who is talking. This does not mean starting a staring contest. In some cultures, direct eye contact is thought of as rude. But if you use direct eye contact in Western culture, it means you are listening.

Avoid Interrupting

To be a good listener, *don't talk*. You cannot listen and talk at the same time. You probably have had the experience of talking with someone who tries to guess what you are going to say. Does that annoy you? If you interrupt people, you'll probably annoy them. Also, you will miss what they are trying to say.

Give Verbal Cues

Respond when you can. **Verbal cues** are short comments that often make people want to continue talking. Many people are looking for support while they talk. Words such as "yes," "I see," "go on," are short and informative. These words let the speaker know that you are tuned in and absorbing the message. Read the case study on the next page. How does Karen use verbal cues?

Case Study

Chung: Yesterday you had a question about the review process for the financial report. I'll give the report to Carmen Banderas tomorrow. Then it will be handed to you. You can add your changes at that time.

Karen: I see.

Chung: Carmen's assistant will input all the changes.

Karen: OK.

Chung: I'll start the review process by giving the report to Carmen.

Karen supplies two verbal cues that communicate information to Chung. Karen says "I see" to support Chung as she gives the information. Then she says "OK" to let Chung know that she is still paying attention.

Give Nonverbal Cues

If you face the person who is talking to you, you show that you are listening.

Nonverbal cues are sometimes called body language. They include nodding, leaning forward, and smiling. Facing the speaker is also a cue that shows you are listening. Your body is positioned to accept the information from the speaker.

Nonverbal cues can also show that you are not listening. Checking your mail or looking out the window shows that you are not paying attention.

Ask Questions to Understand the Message

People will not mind if you ask questions. Most people like it when you ask questions. However, do not interrupt the speaker to ask a question. Wait until the speaker has completed his or her thoughts. Then ask. Questions show interest and help you get the information you need.

Summarize

To **summarize** means to repeat key points. This helps you make sure that everyone is clear about what has been said. Before ending a conversation, summarize. If your supervisor tells you that five different projects should be completed this week, summarize that list of projects. Often, a summary can clear up misunderstandings, as shown in the following case study.

As you summarize the key points of a meeting, you might clear up confusion for others in the meeting.

Case Study

At the marketing meeting, Amy said to Pedro and Helen: "The summer is a peak sales time for the company. We will need to increase the number of people who we call this week. I have reviewed our calling schedule, and I have come up with a plan. Let's make thirty phone calls a day." Pedro and Helen think they understand Amy and they nod in agreement. They do not ask any questions and are about to leave the meeting. Amy provides a summary before Pedro and Helen leave. She says, "Thanks. I think that this week we can each manage thirty calls a day."

Pedro says, "Thirty? I thought you meant ten calls each! Can you help us come up with a plan to organize our time?"

Helen says, "Amy, I would also appreciate some advice from you about reorganizing my work tasks."

Amy provides a summary at the end of the meeting. She repeats the number of calls that they each need to make. If she had not provided a summary, Pedro and Helen would have been confused. The group would not have completed the work that was required.

If you practice your listening skills, they will become routine for you. You might even find yourself using good listening skills without thinking about them.

Comprehension Check

Complete the following exercises. Refer to the lesson if necessary.

A. List two examples of verbal cues.

1. _____

2. _____

B. List three nonverbal cues that show you are listening.

1. _____

2. _____

3. _____

C. Complete the following sentences. Circle the letter in front of the answer.

1. If you don't focus on your listener, you might

    a. shut out everything else.

    b. miss important information.

    c. give verbal cues.

2. If you are talking, you cannot be

    a. listening.

    b. summarizing.

    c. giving verbal cues.

3. If you say, "I understand that you're asking me to complete it by Friday," you are

    a. summarizing.

    b. avoiding interruptions.

    c. giving nonverbal cues.

4. If you are asking questions to understand the speaker's message, do not

    a. interrupt the speaker.

    b. make eye contact.

    c. give nonverbal cues.

Answer the questions after each case study. Then talk about your answers with your partner or group.

Case A

Andy is so worried about his monthly sales report for Mr. Garcia that he does not pay attention to Mr. Garcia's instructions. Although Andy prepares a well-written report, he does not include information about costs, which Mr. Garcia told him to include.

What listening skills would have been the most helpful for Andy?

_____

_____

Case B

Jan and Mark carpool to work. Mark is late again. Finally, Mark arrives. He starts to say something about how his baby had a fever and he did not sleep, but he does not finish his sentence. Jan says, "It seems like your alarm isn't working right." Then she sees the puzzled look on Mark's face.

Why did Mark look puzzled? What did Jan do to cause the confusion?

_____

_____

_____

Case C

Ethan, Mario, and Carol agreed to bring something for Friday night when they would be working late to complete a project. Each of them brought sandwiches. No one brought plates, napkins, or drinks.

What skill would be most important the next time they decide to make such plans?

_____

Case D

Jennifer is the manager of four leasing agents at a rental company. Carter is a leasing agent. He has some important information for Jennifer about a new client. Jennifer invites Carter to her office to discuss the new client. She says she is very interested. As Carter begins to talk, Jennifer starts to look for something in her file drawer. Her back is turned toward him. Carter pauses for a moment, but Jennifer tells him to continue. Carter starts to speak again when Jennifer exclaims, "I found it!"

1. If you were Carter, would you feel like Jennifer was listening? Why or why not?

   _____

   _____

2. Describe Jennifer's body language and how it affected Carter as he spoke.

   _____

   _____

ACT IT OUT

Find a partner. Assign roles as "listener" and "speaker." The speaker will tell the listener about a past job interview. The listener should ask questions occasionally. The listener should listen closely and focus on what the speaker says. The listener should also keep his or her book closed. When the speaker finishes, the listener should open his or her book. The listener should summarize what the speaker said. Use the following subjects to guide the conversation:

- the kind of company it was
- what the job was
- what the room looked like
- whether the speaker got the job

Switch roles and repeat the activity. Discuss the skills you used to listen to your speaker.

Think and Apply

How well do you use the skills in this lesson? Complete these exercises.

A. Think about what you learned in this lesson and answer the questions. Share your answers with your partner or your class.

1. Identify someone in your family, office, or class who is a good listener. What makes you think he or she is a good listener?

   _____

   _____

2. Think about a time when someone interrupted you. How did that make you feel?

   _____

   _____

B. Review your answers to A. Complete the checklist. Then answer the questions that follow.

1. Read the list of skills. Check the boxes next to your strengths.

   ☐ focusing

   ☐ making eye contact

   ☐ not interrupting

   ☐ giving verbal cues

   ☐ giving nonverbal cues

   ☐ asking questions

   ☐ summarizing

2. Do you want to improve any of your skills? Which ones?

   _____

   _____

3. How do you plan to improve the skills you listed in question 2?

   _____

   _____

Lesson 2

Asking the Right Questions

Why do people have misunderstandings in the workplace?

When you are listening to a coworker, how do you ask questions about things that confuse you?

How can you avoid misunderstandings?

Speaking up and asking the right questions can help you avoid misunderstandings in the workplace.

You often rely on others in the workplace to get the information you need to do your job. But sometimes people confuse each other with the things that they say. If you don't understand what someone has said, ask questions. Asking the right questions can help you clear up misunderstandings. It can also help you to avoid problems or to solve problems once they occur.

Avoid Misunderstandings

The people who you work with rely on you to do your job. You rely on the information from others to understand what you need to do. Asking questions is the best way to get this information. Suppose you are being interviewed or starting a new job. You need to ask questions about your job tasks to understand the position. Suppose you are working on a work team to solve a problem. Ask questions to be sure you understand your role on the team and how you can help solve the problem. When people in a group don't understand something, they sometimes don't ask questions to help them understand. Not asking questions creates misunderstandings and confusion.

Some people are shy. They aren't comfortable asking questions. They may think others expect them to know all of the answers. However, asking questions shows you are thoughtful. You can prove that you are genuinely interested in solving the problem or learning the skill or process. In addition, your questions might help avoid potential problems. If you ask the right questions, you learn information that you need to do your job. Read the following case study. Do the workers ask the right questions?

Case Study

Rolando and Brian work in the warehouse of an office supply corporation. They perform many tasks, including taking inventory, labeling stock, and loading delivery trucks. This morning they are working on the stock inventory. Their supervisor, Manoa, tells them that she needs labels on 1,000 boxes containing personal computers.

Brian: What time do you need the labeling finished? Can we finish this inventory first?

Manoa: Sure, there's no big rush.

Rolando: This inventory is going to take quite a while. Do the computers have to go out today?

Manoa: Yes, they do. They've got to be loaded and shipped this afternoon. I guess you'd better do the labeling first. I'm glad you guys are on top of things.

Notice Brian's and Rolando's questions. Brian asks two questions to find out which task they should finish first. The supervisor says "no big rush." Rolando asks a question about what needs to go out today. After Rolando's question, Manoa realizes that she needs to provide a better answer. Rolando's question helps to focus the group's tasks. With more information, the group can focus on the task that must be done right away. By asking for more specific information, Rolando and Brian prevent a possible problem. Their supervisor compliments them on their ability to think ahead.

Ask questions to make sure you understand new information.

Avoid Communication Barriers

It would be nice to think that everyone in every workplace communicates clearly all the time. However, communication doesn't always go smoothly. Sometimes there are **communication barriers.** Communication barriers are factors that block the flow of information. People may talk too fast. They may use **slang,** which is informal language that can be confusing. People also use **jargon,** which includes technical terms that workers may or may not understand. Jargon is language that is specific to a certain type of work or industry. For example, hospital employees use the word "stat" to mean right away. "Stat" is an example of hospital jargon. Sometimes the confusion is not just the words but the directions. Your coworkers or supervisor may be vague and not give complete directions. Ask for an explanation or definition for words or ideas you do not understand.

Ask for Clarification

When listening, think carefully about the information you are getting. If the information is complex, you may want to ask the speaker to repeat. If there is a point you don't understand, ask the speaker to clarify. To **clarify** means to make clear or understandable. When you ask a question, try to identify the specific point you didn't understand. Read about how Tanya asks questions.

Case Study

Tanya is training to become a product assembler at an electrical equipment company. On her first day, she watches teams of workers putting together products on an assembly line. Each worker on the line has a separate task to perform. At the end of the line, the product is complete. Tanya has learned a lot on her first day of training, but she is confused about how she fits into the "big picture." During a break, she speaks to her supervisor, LaDonna.

In some manufacturing companies, product assemblers need to understand every position on the assembly line.

LaDonna: Tomorrow you'll be assigned to one of the assembly teams. Do you have any questions so far?

Tanya: I was wondering if they're going to show me how to do just one task. Will I always be doing the same task?

LaDonna: Well, yes, at first. Then, you'll be trained in each position on the line.

Tanya: Will I be able to handle any position on the line?

LaDonna: Yes. When someone is sick or a new person is training, you will be able to shift to fill any position.

Tanya asked the questions that affected her most directly. Notice that by asking two simple questions, she received information about her future in the company.

Asking questions is a valuable skill in the workplace. With the right information, you can avoid misunderstanding and perform your role.

Comprehension Check

Complete the following exercises. Refer to the lesson if necessary.

A. List three things you can do when you need additional information on the job.

1. _____

2. _____

3. _____

B. List two of the possible effects of asking the right questions.

1. _____

2. _____

C. List three factors that block the flow of information.

1. _____

2. _____

3. _____

D. Mark the following statements T (True) or F (False).

_____ 1. Jargon is an example of a communication barrier.

_____ 2. Asking questions can help you avoid misunderstandings.

_____ 3. *To clarify* means to "use slang."

_____ 4. Asking a question shows that you are foolish.

_____ 5. In the workplace you rarely need information from others to do your job.

_____ 6. If you do not ask questions, you will not understand your job responsibilities.

_____ 7. Asking questions shows that you are thoughtful.

_____ 8. You do not need information from your coworkers to perform on a team.

Answer the questions following each case. Then talk about your answers with your partner or group.

Case A

Tamara and Henry are assigned the task of making telephone calls to survey more than 200 businesses. They have several days to complete the job. They decide to split the call list evenly between them. By the lunch break, Tamara has completed about a quarter of her phone list. Henry has only completed twelve calls.

If you were Henry, what would you ask Tamara about her success with making the calls?

_____

_____

_____

Case B

Jacob and Alanya are technicians at a computer software company. The company has purchased a new building. Many employees will have private offices in the new place. New furniture will also be purchased. Jacob and Alanya have heard rumors about the move. They meet with their supervisor to learn more about the move and the new office space.

Think of three good questions for Jacob and Alanya. Phrase your questions so that you will get the most complete answers possible.

_____

_____

_____

Case C

Samantha is starting her first day as a machine tool operator. She is being trained to use tools like drills and punches to make specialized parts for airplane and truck engines. Brenda is teaching Samantha to use the tools to make the parts. Brenda says, "Remember that some of the bore sizes are one thousandth of an inch. You must be very careful to make the holes just the right size. Follow your blueprints carefully. Ask me if you need to adjust your feed and speeds. After you learn this process, you might have the opportunity to move to the CAD-CAM area." Samantha is listening carefully, but she does not understand all of the words that Brenda is using to describe the job.

1. List the words that might be confusing for Samantha. What is this type of language called?

_____

_____

2. Write at least three questions that Samantha should ask Brenda about the words.

_____

_____

_____

ACT IT OUT

Work with a partner. Take turns role-playing a customer and a worker at an airport rental desk. The customer needs directions to two locations. The rental agent must clarify where the customer wants to go, when he or she needs to be there, and whether the customer would prefer the quickest possible route or the "scenic" route. The rental agent must also clarify whether the customer wants the directions to the two locations to be based on compass directions, landmarks, or a combination. The rental agent provides the customer with clear directions and a map of the area. The customer should ask the clerk to clarify or repeat if necessary. Then, switch roles and repeat the activity.

Think and Apply

How well do you use the skills in this lesson? Complete these exercises.

A. Think about what you learned in this lesson and answer the questions. Share your answers with your partner or your class.

1. Choose a subject that you would like to know more about. It could be a hobby or a procedure at work that is unfamiliar to you. Write at least three questions about that subject.

   _____

   _____

   _____

2. Think about a time that you misunderstood something that someone was trying to tell you. What was unclear? What questions might have helped you get the information you needed?

   _____

   _____

B. Review your answers to A. Complete the checklist. Then answer the questions that follow.

1. Read the list of skills. Check the boxes next to your strengths.

   ☐ asking questions to avoid misunderstandings

   ☐ asking for definitions of unfamiliar words or ideas

   ☐ asking questions that identify specific points or directions that I didn't understand

   ☐ asking the speaker to repeat the information

2. Do you want to improve any of your skills? Which ones?

   _____

   _____

3. How do you plan to improve the skills you listed in question 2?

   _____

Giving Clear Directions; Getting Clear Directions

Clear directions help you perform your job and work with others successfully.

In the workplace, the ability to give and receive clear directions is important for good communication. Every worker needs directions to do his or her job well. Workers need to know what to do, when to do it, and how to do it. In some jobs, giving unclear directions— or not following directions exactly—can be dangerous. For example, a forklift operator must follow careful directions when using machinery. If the directions are not followed, the operator could hurt herself or other people. Not everyone has a job like a forklift operator. However, giving and getting clear directions are a part of every job.

Consider Your Listener

Your listener relies on you for directions and information. One way to give clear directions is by using an object or a drawing that shows what you mean. **Visual aids** are tools like maps, charts, blueprints, simple drawings, and diagrams. By looking at a picture or graphic, a listener can more easily understand what the speaker is trying to say.

Everyone has a point of view. Your **point of view** is the way that you look at something. It is your unique way of understanding information. When two people talk, the speaker has a point of view and the listener has a point of view. Suppose that you are explaining something to a child. You might use simple words and ideas to help the child understand. When you provide information to an experienced coworker, you can usually be brief. Suppose that your listener is a confused customer or patient. In that case, you may need to provide more detailed directions. Try to give directions that your listener will understand. Here's an example.

Case Study

Hakeem is a medical technician at City Hospital. Part of his job involves drawing blood from patients at their homes. One of his patients today is a man who has been experiencing chest pains. The patient is nervous and upset.

Hakeem: Mr. Edwards, the doctor wants to make sure there's nothing to worry about. I'm going to take a blood sample from you.

Mr. Edwards: Why should the doctor be worried? Hey, what are you doing?

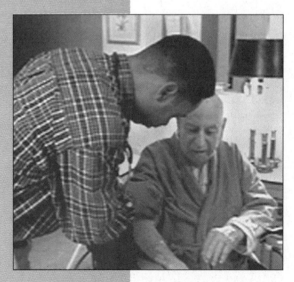

Some of your listeners may require careful and detailed directions from you.

Hakeem: Before we draw your blood, we need to make sure you're not anemic. Anemia is a health problem where the blood doesn't contain enough iron. I'm going to prick your finger with this needle. It will sting for just a second. You will need to stay still. Look away from the needle or close your eyes if you need to. Please don't be nervous, Mr. Edwards. I would like you to relax and lie back. We'll be finished in just a few minutes.

Hakeem realizes that Mr. Edwards is worried about his condition. First, Hakeem explains the procedure for taking blood. Second, Hakeem tells Mr. Edwards to remain still, relax, and lie back. He tells Mr. Edwards that he does not need to look at the needle if that will help. Hakeem provides specific and careful directions for Mr. Edwards.

Get the Information You Need

Active listeners ask questions, take notes, and focus on information.

There are several things you can do to make sure you receive clear directions in the workplace. You can ask questions to help you to **interpret** or understand information. Suppose that you need to move a heavy box through a warehouse. You ask your supervisor where to put the box. He is writing a report and doesn't seem to be listening to you. He waves toward the far end of the building and says, "Put it over there." If you aren't sure where he means, it's up to you to ask for more explanation: "Do you mean over there next to the main exit?"

To make sure you get clear directions, be an active listener. Focus your attention on the information you are given. You may want to take notes or draw a picture or diagram to help you remember the information. Sometimes it helps to repeat aloud what a supervisor or coworker tells you. Or you can paraphrase. **Paraphrasing** means repeating the same information in your own words. Suppose your speaker gives you a long description of the sales plans for an upcoming business trip. To paraphrase, you might say, "It sounds as if it will be a busy trip" or "So you believe that you will be more successful on the West Coast." Paraphrasing is an excellent way to make sure you really understand. If you have misunderstood, your supervisor or coworker can correct you immediately.

Look at how Glen paraphrases and interprets his boss's instructions.

Case Study

Glen works as a plumber's apprentice. He is new to the job and there is a lot to learn. Soraya is friendly and she's a good plumber. But Glen has to pay close attention to what she says. When she's in a hurry, she's sometimes not very clear. Today Soraya is about to check the leak in a pipe in the ceiling of an office building.

Soraya: You're going to have to shut off the water, Glen.

Glen: Do you mean the main water valve?

Soraya: That's right. I need the water shut off in the whole building.

Glen: Okay. I'd better tell the maintenance technician that I need to go in the basement. How long should I tell her the water will be off?

Soraya: Good question. Tell her we'll need half an hour.

Glen interpreted Soraya's comments correctly. He used common sense to figure out that people don't enjoy being without water. He asks Soraya how long the water will be off. Then, he can give the same information to the customer. By asking how long the water will be off, he is getting the information he needs to keep the customer informed.

You will use directions throughout your career. The way that you give directions affects how others work with you. Using directions to complete your job tasks and learn new skills can help you improve as an employee.

Comprehension Check

Complete the following exercises. Refer to the lesson if necessary.

A. List three examples of visual aids.

1. _____

2. _____

3. _____

B. List two ways to receive clear directions.

1. _____

2. _____

C. Complete the following sentences using the list of words.

point of view   visual aid
paraphrasing   interpreting

1. If you consider your listener's experience, you are considering

   his or her _____.

2. Repeating your speaker's message in your own words is a

   form of _____.

3. Larisa is having trouble explaining a heating system to Sam.
   She draws a sketch. This is an example of a

   _____.

D. Mark the following statements T (True) or F (False).

_____ 1. Clear directions are important only when you're new
            on the job.

_____ 2. An experienced coworker has a different point of view
            than a new employee.

_____ 3. Interpreting directions means repeating the directions
            in your own words.

_____ 4. Visual aids are helpful for explaining directions.

Answer the questions following each case. Then talk about your answers with your partner or group.

Case A

Raul and Magda work in a public library. Magda is late for work and misses this morning's staff meeting. When she arrives, Raul tells her she has been given the task of sending out overdue book notices with him. They need to use a computer to write the notices. Raul tells Magda how to perform the task. He speaks very quickly and ends with, "OK. Let's get started." Magda rolls her eyes and says, "I didn't understand a word you just said."

1. What might Magda have done to understand Raul's directions?

   _____

   _____

2. What could Raul do to show Magda how to perform the task?

   _____

   _____

Case B

Janelle is a receptionist at a veterinarian's office. She handles the front desk, does filing, and sets up appointments. She also helps customers fill out forms. Ms. Contreras wants to order ID tags for her three dogs. Janelle hands Ms. Contreras three forms, one for each dog. Janelle also gives Ms. Contreras a copy of a completed form Ms. Contreras can refer to if she is confused about anything.

1. What communication method did Janelle use for Ms. Contreras?

   _____

2. Why do you think Janelle used this technique?

   _____

Case C

Rob and Jason are telemarketers. They sell children's videos by phone to movie stores and schools. They also organize brochures and mail them to customers who are interested in learning about the videos. During a lunch break, Jason tells Rob how busy next week will be. Following is Jason's story about next week.

I talked to a customer today and he would like to order ten videos. But he would like to read about the different programs before buying them. So, next week I will need to organize ten different brochures for that customer. I'll mail those next Tuesday. Then a woman from Florida called. She said that she viewed one of the programs at a store and would like to order it. She remembered the characters in the program but could not remember the title. So, I will need to describe the program to Mary today and ask her for the title. Then I need to call that woman in Florida next week. I hope to mail her one brochure next Thursday.

Paraphrase Jason's work story. Include only the information about what Jason needs to do next week.

_____

_____

_____

ACT IT OUT

Work with a partner. One of you will play the role of a supervisor. The other will be the worker. Choose a work task, such as logging onto a computer, using a copier, or replacing supplies. The supervisor must give directions to the worker on how to perform the chosen work task. The worker must ask questions to clarify any confusing information. Use any of the communication techniques from the lesson, including visual aids, paraphrasing, and interpreting. Choose another work task and switch roles. Repeat the activity.

Think and Apply

How well do you use the skills in this lesson? Complete these exercises.

A. Think about what you learned in this lesson and answer the questions. Share your answers with your partner or your class.

1. Write directions to a specific place. Write at least three sentences.

   _____

   _____

   _____

2. Think about a time when you didn't understand a work or school task. How did you interpret the directions? What could you have done to receive clearer directions?

   _____

   _____

B. Review your answers to A. Complete the checklist. Then answer the questions that follow.

1. Read the list of skills. Check the boxes next to your strengths.

   ☐ using visual aids

   ☐ considering the listener's point of view

   ☐ interpreting the speaker's directions correctly

   ☐ repeating the speaker's words

   ☐ paraphrasing

2. Do you want to improve any of your skills? Which ones?

   _____

   _____

3. How do you plan to improve the skills you listed in question 2?

   _____

   _____

Lesson 4

Giving a Clear Message

How do the words you choose affect the listener?

What do your body movements and facial expressions say about you?

Your word choice and body language affect your message.

Have you ever said something and been surprised by the reaction? People may not understand you for many reasons. One reason may be that you use certain words incorrectly. Or your body language may be confusing to your listener. You may give nonverbal cues that don't agree with your words. If your body language and your words work together, you'll communicate more clearly.

Pay Attention to Your Vocabulary

To give clear messages, pay attention to your **vocabulary** or the words you use. Choose your words carefully. For instance, if you are giving a positive message, you need to use positive words. Read the example.

Dana is the manager of a large cafeteria. She asks one of the employees, Pete, to clean the stockroom. He straightens up the shelves, throws away the trash, and sweeps and mops the floor. Dana wants to congratulate Pete, so she says, "You did not do a bad job at all." Pete feels puzzled because he thinks that he has done a very good job cleaning the stockroom.

Giving positive messages to employees is one way to create a pleasant work environment.

Why is Pete puzzled? Dana used negative sounding words, "not" and "bad." If Dana had said, "You did a great job," Pete would feel appreciated for his hard work.

Sometimes you have to give negative messages to workers. It's important to choose your words carefully when giving these messages. For example, imagine that Pete forgot to clean one of the tables in the stockroom. Pete would feel upset if Dana said, "You always forget to do part of the work. Get in there and finish!" It is better to combine praise with criticism. If Dana says, "You did a good job on the floor, but you still need to finish the table in the corner," Pete can feel good about the work he did correctly. However, he also knows that he has to clean the table to finish the job. By avoiding harsh words, you can communicate negative messages without upsetting people.

Be careful to use the correct word. Sometimes a word can have more than one meaning. Suppose Tim just gave an employee, Max, directions on how to drive to a customer's office building. Max is repeating the directions back to Tim to make sure he understands them.

Max: First I drive north on the expressway. I get off at Kramer and go left on Kramer.

Tim: Yes.

Max: Then at the corner of Kramer and Burnet I turn left on Burnet.

Tim: Right.

Max: OK. I turn right on Burnet.

Tim: No. You turn left on Burnet.

Tim confused Max because he used the word *right* to mean "correct." Max thought he meant the direction. Make sure to use words with more than one meaning carefully.

Pay Attention to Your Body Language

Your **nonverbal messages** are your body language. The ways that you move convey messages. Your body language tells your listener a lot about what you think. Most people notice your gestures and make judgments based on them. For instance, if you are talking to someone who is slumped in her chair, you may think that she's bored or unhappy. Problems can arise when your body language doesn't match your words. When body language does not agree with the words spoken, people are more likely to believe what they see rather than what they hear.

You can use body language to make a good impression. If you want to show confidence, try to do the following:

- Stand, walk, and talk proudly.

- Look people directly in the eye.

- Have a firm handshake.

Presenting a positive image can help you at work. If you are friendly and open, most people will feel comfortable talking and working with you. Body language is an important part of making our communication effective. The following case study shows how good body language improves communication.

Case Study

Recently, Claire interviewed for a job as a receptionist at a health clinic. She got to the office 10 minutes early to show that she was punctual. As she waited for her interview, she sat straight and skimmed some reading material in the office. When Mr. Lockhart came to greet her, she smiled and extended her hand for a firm handshake. During the interview, she smiled and looked directly at him as she spoke. She was careful not to fiddle with her pen or purse strap. She took care to speak carefully and not too fast.

It is important to present a positive image during a job interview.

What kind of impression did Claire give? How did she use nonverbal cues to send a message? Do you think her body language helped her get the job?

To avoid giving mixed messages, try to say what you really mean. Use positive words for positive messages. If your message is negative, be sensitive and specific about your complaints. Be careful to use words correctly, too. Also try to match your words with your body language. This will be easy in most situations when you are sure of yourself and sure of the people around you. Then you feel free to show as well as tell what you think. Your body language goes right along with what you are saying.

Comprehension Check

Complete the following exercises. Refer to the lesson if necessary.

A. Mark the following statements T (True) or F (False).

_____ 1. Giving clear messages means waiting for someone to ask a question.

_____ 2. Self-confident people stand and walk tall.

_____ 3. Your nonverbal messages should match your verbal messages in job situations only.

_____ 4. When a speaker's verbal and nonverbal messages don't match, the communication is clear.

B. Answer the following questions. Circle the letter in front of the answer.

1. How can you avoid upsetting people when you need to deliver negative messages?

   a. Avoid harsh words.
   b. Shake hands firmly.
   c. Spell words correctly.

2. Which of the following is an example of an effective positive message?

   a. "Well, at least you did that right."
   b. "I guess you performed pretty well."
   c. "Your memo is well-written."

3. Which of the following is not an example of self-confidence?

   a. standing and walking proudly
   b. moving your hands nervously while talking
   c. looking someone directly in the eye

4. Which of the following words and body language do not agree?

   a. saying "Nice to meet you" and shaking someone's hand
   b. saying "I'm interested in what you are saying" and writing a letter at the same time
   c. focusing on your computer and saying "I'm busy now"

Answer the questions after each case. Then talk about your answers with your partner or group.

Case A

After moving to a new city, Seth visited a local bank to open a savings and checking account. He talked with Batina, a customer service representative, for about thirty minutes. Batina started the conversation by saying, "What can I do for you?" While Seth asked questions, Batina looked at her watch, looked out the window, and read something on her bulletin board. She gave Seth brief answers to his questions. He thanked her and left puzzled.

What was confusing about Batina's behavior? How should she have behaved when Seth asked questions?

_____

_____

_____

_____

Case B

Wanda is the computer technician for a medical supply company. She makes sure the employees' computers work properly. Last week, Sean's computer kept crashing. When Wanda arrived in his office, she sat down and began working. She didn't ask Sean for any information. When Sean tried to explain the problem, she stared straight at the monitor. Wanda moved her chair so Sean was looking directly at her back.

What does Wanda's body language say to Sean? How should Wanda behave when she works with a client?

_____

_____

_____

Case C

Gail is a sales clerk at a gift and card shop. Molly is the store manager. Gail is in the stockroom unloading packages of wedding invitations. She needs to check the shipping invoice and input the information in the computer. Then she will stock the packages on a shelf. Gail is working slowly but carefully. She has not performed these tasks before, and she wants to do them correctly. Molly walks into the stockroom to check Gail's progress. Molly speaks quickly.

Molly: OK. Are you about done with the unpacking? Then the inputting. I forgot to tell you we need to call the customers, too. OK? Good. I'll check back later.

Molly leaves the room. Gail is confused. She thinks that she needs to work more quickly, but she is not sure about the order of the tasks.

How would you describe Molly's message? Are her directions clear? Why or why not?

_____

_____

TALK IT OUT

Find a partner. Take turns interviewing each other. Ask your partner questions about his or her job experience and interests. Ask:

- What do you like to do?
- What kind of jobs have you had?
- What are your skills?
- What have you studied in school?

Answer the questions. Be aware of the nonverbal messages you are giving. Pay careful attention to the following:

- posture
- eye contact
- gestures
- facial expression

Evaluate each other's body language and spoken words. Write three words that describe your partner's body language. Share them with your partner.

Think and Apply

How well do you use the skills in this lesson? Complete these exercises.

A. Think about what you learned in the lesson and answer the questions. Share your answers with your partner or your class.

1. Pay careful attention to your word choice during the next week. Keep a record of any positive and negative messages in a notebook. How did you provide positive messages? Negative messages?

   _____

   _____

2. Notice your body language during the next week. What do you tell people about yourself with your body movements? Write a few sentences that describe what others might think of your body language.

   _____

   _____

B. Review your answers to A. Complete the checklist. Then answer the questions that follow.

1. Read the list of skills. Check the boxes next to your strengths.
   - ☐ using positive words when giving a positive message
   - ☐ using words with several meanings carefully
   - ☐ avoiding harsh words when giving a negative message
   - ☐ showing confidence in myself
   - ☐ being aware of my body language
   - ☐ matching my body language to my words

2. Do you want to improve any of your skills? Which ones?

   _____

3. How do you plan to improve the skills you listed in question 2?

   _____

Working with Different Styles

How would you describe the way you work within a group?

Do you speak up or are you more comfortable listening?

Knowing how to work with people with different work styles will help you do your job well.

You come across many different working styles every day. You work with your family to complete household activities and create special events. Your friends and coworkers count on you to make plans and meet goals. As a member of many groups, you know that each person has a different style of working. Some people like to "take charge" and lead the group. Other people may sit through many meetings without saying a word. The most successful groups work together to reach common goals. And the most successful workers learn how to work well with all types of working styles. This lesson will teach you about different styles and how to work with each style.

Understand Different Work Styles

Offices, restaurants, and schools are made up of people who come together to complete goals. In an office, a clerk may ask a coworker for help in updating a file system. Hosts in restaurants may find out about the number of available tables by asking staff. In school, a student may lead a group to finish a classroom project on time. Each member brings unique talents and ideas. The group combines talents to meet the goals.

To work well with other people, it is helpful to understand three different work styles. The **aggressive** work style is a forceful way of working. The aggressive person often takes charge of a group and may try to make decisions for others. **Passive** people often stay in the background and let other people make decisions for them. An assertive working style is a confident way of working. **Assertive** means bold and confident. Assertive people are comfortable offering an idea or opinion. However, they also listen to others' ideas. These working styles are present in most workplaces. Is Josh aggressive, passive, or assertive in this example?

Case Study

Josh is an apprentice photographer at a studio. The studio produces pictures of furniture for catalogs and magazines. Josh sets up the furniture, lights, and camera for Hannah, the photographer. After Josh sets up a picture, Hannah steps up to the camera. However, this time Josh notices that the light on the sofa does not look right and makes a suggestion for improving the photograph.

Josh: Hannah, I think the light on the sofa may be too harsh. I have an idea for making it look warmer.

Hannah: I see. Would you show me your idea?

Every successful group effort is made up of the individual talents of the group members.

How would you describe the way Josh participates? Do you think he acts aggressively, passively, or assertively? Josh expresses an interest in his work. He thinks of a way to get involved in the creation of the photograph. By speaking up, he lets Hannah know that he has a good idea. He does not blurt his idea out, but asks her if she would like to hear it. He makes an effort to improve their work. Hannah appreciates Josh's idea, and she gives him the chance to try his idea.

If Josh had been too aggressive and said, "Let me fix this. I think I could do it much better than you," Hannah might have responded differently. She might have been offended or upset by Josh's remarks. She might think that Josh didn't respect her. She would not have appreciated his idea. If Josh had kept his idea to himself, he might have regretted it later because he would have missed the chance to learn and help. Also, Hannah would never have known that Josh had an idea.

No one is assertive all of the time. Sometimes you may choose to be quiet, and at other times you may want to contribute. During the quieter times, listen and respect the opinions of others.

To show that you are listening, face your speaker and wait until that person has finished speaking.

Use Your Interpersonal Skills

Interpersonal skills are the abilities to relate and work with other people. Listening carefully, speaking politely, and being friendly are effective interpersonal skills for the workplace.

If someone in a group is speaking, don't interrupt. Wait until that person has finished speaking before you speak. Listen carefully. Then respond. Let everyone offer ideas. If someone in your group is quiet, you may choose to ask for that person's opinions, thoughts, and ideas.

Everyone has a point of view. As you learned in Lesson 3, a **point of view** is the position from which someone considers something.

If you are too aggressive and force your point of view onto other people, you will not accomplish much in a group. Your coworkers will not appreciate being ignored or being told what to do. They may become angry. When you work in a group, consider different points of view. Do Sarah and Will appreciate each other's point of view?

Case Study

Sarah and Will work at a zoo, and they are in charge of hiring part-time summer workers. They would like to post signs advertising a job fair that will occur in May.

Will: I think we should put the ads on the bulletin board in the staff lunchroom. I don't think people visiting the zoo would be interested in these jobs.

Sarah: That's a good idea. But I think putting the ads up in the zoo would attract many new workers. Maybe we could put them at the entrance? When I worked at a theme park we did that, and the park had a good turnout for the job fair.

Will: That's a good idea. We should post them there, too.

Will and Sarah use their interpersonal skills well. They listen carefully to each other. Sarah expresses her idea after Will has spoken. Will shows Sarah that he appreciates her good idea. Sarah's suggestion is based on her point of view and experience. When she worked at the theme park, she learned how to find new workers. Will benefits because Sarah shares her unique experiences and talents with him.

Working with people with different work styles is a challenge. The way you approach your group and the way you perform will affect how well your group works together.

Comprehension Check

Complete the following exercises. Refer to the lesson if necessary.

A. List the three types of working styles.

1. _____

2. _____

3. _____

B. List three interpersonal skills.

1. _____

2. _____

3. _____

C. Complete the following sentences. Circle the letter in front of the answer.

1. When Sam asks Domingo for his thoughts during a project meeting, Domingo looks away and says he does not have any good ideas. Domingo has

   a. an aggressive working style.
   b. an assertive working style.
   c. a passive working style.

2. A law firm purchased a new copier machine. When the machine was running, it was noisy. Stella said she needed a quiet work environment, and the machine should be placed near Pat's department. Pat thought the machine should be placed near Stella's department because his department didn't use a copier very much. Both Stella and Pat were considering their own

   a. points of view.
   b. interpersonal skills.
   c. working styles.

Answer the questions following each case. Then talk about your answers with your partner or group.

Case A

Alice, Marisa, and Lukas are working on a list of questions for their phone sales. They will make calls to sell the lawn services of their company. Marisa believes she has some great ideas. She talks during the entire meeting and does not let anyone else contribute. At the end of the meeting, Lukas and Alice agree with Marisa's ideas, but they regret that they did not contribute any of their own.

1. What is Marisa's work style? What are the work styles of Lukas and Alice?

   _____

   _____

2. How could the group members improve their work styles?

   _____

   _____

Case B

Theo and Rafael create graphics for a small neighborhood magazine. Theo has worked for the company for five years. Rafael has worked at the company for one month. Rafael has good ideas, but he has some difficulty explaining them. During Monday morning's staff meeting, Theo becomes frustrated with Rafael. Theo does not have the patience to wait for Rafael to complete his sentences. So, rather than wait, Theo interrupts Rafael four times during the meeting.

What do you think of Theo's behavior? What skills could he improve?

   _____

   _____

Case C

Officer Pullman arrives at the scene of a minor car accident. No one is hurt, but he needs to ask some questions and complete an accident report. Kelly's car is on the grass on the side of the road. Larry's car is still in the intersection. Officer Pullman asks Kelly what happened.

Kelly: I was traveling east through the intersection. The light was green, but there was a big van in the left lane. I could not see his car because of the van. He turned right into me. He hit me and I veered off the road onto the grass.

Officer Pullman: Thank you, Kelly. Larry, would you please tell me your account of what happened?

Larry: I was traveling west. I pulled out into the intersection to look at the oncoming traffic. That van was pulled way over so I couldn't see. I thought the lane was clear and I started to turn. She was coming through the intersection. That was when the accident happened.

1. How are Kelly and Larry describing the accident to Officer Pullman?

   _____

2. Do Kelly's account and Larry's account have anything in common? Explain why or why not.

   _____

   _____

TALK IT OUT

Work with another student. Discuss some of the working styles with which you are familiar. Talk about work, school, or home situations. Are there situations when it would be better to be passive? To be assertive? To be aggressive? Share your ideas with the rest of the class.

Think and Apply

How well do you use the skills in this lesson? Complete these exercises.

A. Think about what you learned in this lesson and answer the questions. Share your answers with your partner or your class.

1. Choose someone who has a different work style from you. How is his or her style different? Describe his or her style.

   _____

   _____

2. Think about a group that you belong to. The group can be at work or home. Write about a disagreement that your group had. How many different points of view were presented? Describe those points of view.

   _____

   _____

   _____

B. Review your answers to A. Complete the checklist. Then answer the questions that follow.

1. Read the list of skills. Check the boxes next to your strengths.
   - ☐ understanding different work styles
   - ☐ using an assertive style
   - ☐ speaking politely, listening carefully, and being friendly
   - ☐ asking the quiet members of my group for their opinions
   - ☐ considering different points of view

2. Do you want to improve any of your skills? Which ones?

   _____

3. How do you plan to improve the skills you listed in question 2?

   _____

   _____

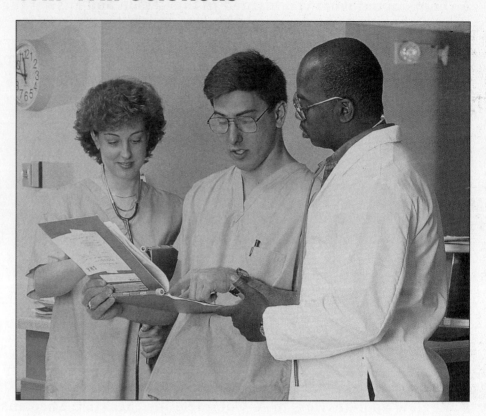

Lesson 6

Negotiating to Achieve Win-Win Solutions

What can you do if the members of your group disagree with each other?

How can you reach a solution that will make everyone happy?

When should you give up something you want so that the entire group can benefit?

Talking through solutions can help you and your coworkers meet goals.

One benefit of working in a group is sharing the ideas of different people. Each person has knowledge that the group needs. However, working in a group can also be a challenge. As you learned in Lessons 3 and 5, each person has a **point of view** or position from which he or she considers something. Group members may have different points of view and may not agree with each other. However, group members need to settle disagreements. So, groups negotiate. **Negotiation** is a way of talking with others to decide how to solve a problem. Each member of a group contributes ideas during a negotiation. The group decides on a solution. Group members should feel happy with a solution because they all helped to negotiate it.

44

Identify Group Goals

To start a negotiation and solve a problem, a group needs to set goals it can meet. For example, suppose that two people share an office. They might like their office files to be organized in the file cabinet at all times. But that goal might be impossible to achieve. Instead, the two workers might decide that their goal is to keep the files they are not using in the cabinet. Their "working" files will be kept out of the cabinet for easy access. There's no point in setting goals that are too hard to reach. In fact, some groups may need to set one goal at a time. As they reach each goal, they'll become more and more confident. Often groups think of more than one plan during negotiation. They try to choose the best plan.

Work Toward Agreement

Groups can settle disagreement with a **compromise.** In a compromise, the members each give something up. One member might give up his or her time in order to complete extra work. Another member might share a personal computer so that others could use it, too. In a compromise, several things must happen. First, group members must figure out why they disagree. Second, each member must listen carefully to the ideas of the other members. The group may also need to gather new facts and information. Then they can discuss what each side must give up for the good of the group. Here's an example.

Case Study

Tasty Bakery ships 2,000 rolls to one of its largest customers every day. However, today an oven had to be repaired during regular baking hours. The bakery was two hours behind. The workers met to discuss the situation.

Mixer: Well, the dough's all set to go, but we can't get it baked in time for the five o'clock rolls delivery.

Baker: But the oven's fixed. We'll catch up.

Mixer: No way. We can't make up two hours!

Packager: Not unless we package the rolls faster. We can't do that unless we have more help.

Baker: I normally clean my work area after giving you the rolls. I can help you with packaging, but then I have to get back to my work. I can't do that if my work area isn't clean.

Mixer: I have to stay in the kitchen to mix some glaze. I can clean your area while the mixing machine is running. I guess we will make it!

To solve a problem, it is often necessary to gather information from the people with whom you work.

The three workers used compromise to meet the group goal of completing the roll order. The workers gave up their normal routine in order to help each other.

Not all problems can be solved by compromising. For example, when the bakery has another emergency, the bakers may not be able to solve it by reorganizing their work. Instead, they may need a more creative solution. **Creative problem-solving** is a way of thinking of alternative and imaginative solutions. Creative problem-solving is necessary when solutions are not readily apparent.

Brainstorming is a creative problem-solving procedure. It is a method used to create new ideas. Group members use their imagination to find solutions that may be unusual. To do this, group members list every solution they can think of. They let one idea lead them to another. During brainstorming, group members accept all ideas. They do not criticize any idea, even if they think a certain idea will not work. Later, the group can choose a solution from the list. Groups use creative problem-solving to reach solutions that are acceptable to everyone. Here's an example.

Case Study

The Long Life Insurance Group has a problem. The company handles about 20,000 new customers a year. The processing department at Long Life must fill out five different forms for each customer. This department cannot keep up with the amount of work. The head of the company, Ms. Patel, holds a staff meeting to discuss ways to process the forms more quickly. During the meeting, several staff members suggest that another department should take over two of the forms. The manager of that department thinks that the staff should work overtime until new people can be hired. No one is happy with these two ideas. The meeting continues and the staff tries to brainstorm to come up with a better solution. Armando, a processing clerk, makes a suggestion.

A brainstorming session is a meeting which provides the group members with an opportunity to suggest as many ideas as possible.

Armando: Instead of using five different forms, why don't we create one form made just for our company? That way all the customer information will be in one place. It'll cut down on paperwork and make filling out the forms quicker.

Ms. Patel: I think Armando has come up with a good solution. What do the rest of you think? How could we design this form?

Armando's suggestion is creative. No one in the group needs to work overtime and no one in another department needs to do extra work. Armando's idea saves the staff time and energy. By brainstorming as a group, the staff solves its problem.

Whenever people work in a group, there will probably be some disagreements. But group members can only succeed by working together. Sometimes just one person's suggestion can lead to major improvements. Everyone must be willing to listen, offer suggestions, and work toward a solution.

Comprehension Check

Complete the following exercise. Refer to the lesson if necessary.

A. List three things people should do in the negotiation process.

1. _____

2. _____

3. _____

B. Mark the following statements T (True) or F (False).

_____ 1. When members of a group give something up for the good of the whole group, the members have compromised.

_____ 2. Brainstorming is a procedure used in creative problem-solving.

C. Complete each sentence. Circle the letter in front of the answer.

1. Negotiation is

   a. a way to perform extra work.
   b. a way to talk with others to solve a problem.
   c. a way to tell other people what to do.

2. Creative problem-solving requires

   a. imagination.
   b. compromise.
   c. an easy plan.

3. During brainstorming, group members

   a. suggest ideas that may be unusual.
   b. choose one member and ask that person to provide one solution.
   c. criticize ideas right away.

4. To resolve a disagreement through compromise, you should first

   a. try to solve it on your own.
   b. determine who is at fault.
   c. determine the reasons for the disagreement.

Answer the questions following each case. Then talk about your answers with your partner or group.

Case A

At Belson Shoes, salespeople work on commission. They get a percentage of the cost of every pair of shoes they sell. For example, a salesperson who gets a 5% commission makes $2.50 for selling a $50 pair of shoes. The salesperson can make twice as much for selling a $100 pair of shoes. Lately, this has been a problem. The salespeople have been showing customers only the most expensive shoes. Several customers have complained that they are left "on their own" if they tell a salesperson they are looking for inexpensive shoes. The general manager doesn't want to discourage employees from trying to make money. However, she wants satisfied customers. She asks her staff to help her brainstorm a solution to this problem.

1. What solutions might come out of a brainstorming session?

   _____

   _____

   _____

2. Why do you think the manager used brainstorming as a way to solve the shoe store's problem?

   _____

   _____

   _____

Case B

National Bank and Trust has had a staff shortage. The flu season hit the company hard. On many days, the bank operates with only half of its regular staff. Tony Celucci, the bank manager, calls an employee meeting. He tells his staff that they must work together to find a solution to the shortages. Avia, a teller, suggests that Tony schedule more employees than needed for each shift. That way if someone calls in sick, enough employees will still be on duty. Allen, a loan officer, says, "I've got another idea. Why don't we have one person 'on-call' each day? If no one's sick, the on-call person gets the day off. But if someone calls in sick, the on-call person comes in to work." Everyone agrees that Allen has a better solution.

What techniques did the bank employees use to figure out a solution to the problem?

_____

_____

TALK IT OUT

Work with a partner. Imagine that you both work for the same store, factory, or office. Create a work schedule for two weeks. You may want to use a calendar. Each of you must work at least 40 hours per week. In addition, you must each work at least three nights and one weekend day a week. You don't have to agree to everything your partner says. If you have a problem with working on Sundays or you have certain nights when you are busy at home, discuss this with your partner. Use compromise and creative problem-solving to work out the schedule. Do not complete the schedule until you reach an agreement. When you finish, discuss these questions with your partner: Did you think of any creative solutions to the scheduling problems? Did you brainstorm? What compromises did each of you have to make?

Think and Apply

How well do you use the skills in this lesson? Complete these exercises.

A. Think about what you learned in this lesson and answer the questions. Share your answers with your partner or class.

1. Discuss with a partner how to reach one of your career goals. What would you need to compromise to reach your goal? Would you have to work more hours to earn money for college or other training? Would you have to sacrifice your free time? With your partner, brainstorm a list of compromises you would be willing to make.

   _____

   _____

2. When was the last time you negotiated for something you wanted? Did you have to compromise anything? Would you say you used creative problem-solving? How would you handle it differently now, using the skills in this lesson?

   _____

   _____

B. Review your answers to A. Complete the checklist. Then answer the questions that follow.

1. Read the list of skills. Check the boxes next to your strengths.

   ☐ negotiating

   ☐ compromising

   ☐ using creative problem-solving

2. Do you want to improve any of your skills? Which ones?

   _____

3. How do you plan to improve the skills you listed in question 2?

   _____

Giving and Accepting Feedback

How do you politely tell other people what you think they should do?

How do you respond when someone is giving you feedback or advice?

How can you improve your work skills by using the feedback from others?

A successful worker uses feedback to learn and teach others.

To communicate well in the workplace, you need to be able to lead and teach. You also need to follow directions and learn. To lead and teach, you provide feedback to others. To follow directions and learn, you accept feedback. Feedback is a two-way form of communication. You will accept feedback from your boss and possibly from your coworkers. You will provide feedback primarily to your coworkers.

There are two types of feedback. **Positive feedback** is praise. It comes in several forms, such as a compliment or a good performance evaluation. **Negative feedback** offers a correction or a suggestion on how you can do better. Negative feedback is also called criticism.

Many people are not comfortable giving and accepting negative feedback. It is important to give negative feedback in as positive a way as possible. Both types of feedback help you improve your overall job skills.

Teach Others by Giving Input

If you are teaching someone else how to do a task, there are a few key things to remember. First, compliment the person when he or she does something right. This encourages that person to do even better. Second, try to avoid giving negative feedback in front of others. No one feels comfortable hearing criticism if another person is listening. To coach someone, you can **model** or demonstrate the task or process yourself. Then have the other person do it after you. If he or she does part of the job correctly, give positive feedback. For example, say "You did that first part very well." This builds up the other person's confidence. It opens up communication so you can then tell the person about areas that need improvement, "You did the first step fine. But try to remember to. . . ." Look at how Rhonda gives feedback.

Positive feedback reinforces or strengthens good job performance.

Case Study

Seamus and Rhonda work on the maintenance crew of a theme park. Among other tasks, they do cleaning, painting, and lawn work. Rhonda is teaching Seamus how to paint one of the theme park's booths. Seamus is not listening carefully because he's eager to get started painting. When he dips his brush into the paint can, white paint drips onto the floor.

Rhonda: OK. That's what happens when you take the paintbrush out of the can too fast. Remember, you want to dip the brush and then wipe it lightly against the inside top of the can. That way the extra paint stays in the can. Try it again. Perfect. Now you've got it.

Rhonda has shown excellent leadership skills. She didn't lose her temper even though Seamus hadn't paid close attention to her directions. Also, she let him know right away when he did the task correctly.

Learn from Others by Accepting Input

If you make a mistake on the job, chances are good that someone will tell you about it. Hopefully, he or she will offer polite criticism. But that isn't always the case. The important thing for you to remember is this: Try not to get defensive or angry. Use feedback as a learning tool. Listen for how you can improve. Never assume that you know a better way when you are new to a job. That kind of knowledge comes with time and experience.

Case Study

Benita is an apprentice operating engineer with the state highway department. Her job requires her to operate several kinds of heavy machinery. Today, Benita's supervisor, Del, is showing her how to operate the bulldozer for the first time.

Del: All right. Now, you have to remember to back down a muddy hill slowly. If you have to brake too quickly, the machine might skid and throw you off balance. You don't ever want to lose control when you're running a machine this big.

Benita: Should I try it now?

Del: Go ahead. Wait! You were backing up too fast. As you get used to it, you'll be able to tell when you're doing it wrong. For now, concentrate on doing it as slowly as you can. There you go. Good work, Benita!

Accepting input from others can help you learn and improve.

There's a lot to learn in a job like Benita's. And not all supervisors are as patient as Del. Imagine if Del had screamed at her, "I told you not to go so fast! Try it again and this time get it right!" By listening constructively, Benita would probably be able to figure out why Del became so angry. After all, he's teaching her to operate a machine that weighs many tons. Del can't allow Benita to make a mistake that might hurt her or someone else. And Benita shouldn't get defensive while learning new skills. The best response to a supervisor's anger would be, "I see what you mean. Okay if I try it again?"

It isn't always easy to respond this way, but it is a good way to learn. Try to filter out the negative feelings and use the information that will help you. Following are some tips to make the feedback work for you:

Allow Yourself Time. Give yourself enough time to correct your performance. Take a moment to make sure you understand the feedback. If you do not understand, ask questions. Then, set a goal to improve your performance based on that feedback.

Make a Plan. If you understand the feedback and are committed to improve, make a plan. You may decide to make a schedule to improve a skill within a week or a year. Make sure you check your performance to see if you achieve your goal.

Get Advice from Coworkers. Some of your coworkers may have received the same type of feedback as you have. You should ask for advice. You might be able to follow a coworker's plan to improve. Suppose you have had trouble operating a piece of machinery. If one of your coworkers also has had experience with that machinery, you might learn from that coworker.

Remember that your coworkers and boss give you feedback to help you. No one knows everything about his or her job. Use feedback as an opportunity to learn and improve. And when you give feedback to others, remember to provide it in a way that you would like to receive it yourself.

Comprehension Check

Complete the following exercises. Refer to the lesson if necessary.

A. List three ways of giving feedback.

1. _____

2. _____

3. _____

B. List two examples of positive feedback.

1. _____

2. _____

C. List three ways that you can use feedback to improve.

1. _____

2. _____

3. _____

D. Why do you think that getting angry is not a useful way to give feedback?

1. _____

2. _____

E. Read each sentence. Circle the letter in front of the answer.

1. Negative feedback is also called

   a. argument.

   b. criticism.

   c. interruption.

2. When you receive negative feedback, what should you do?

   a. interrupt

   b. pretend you know better

   c. listen constructively

Answer the questions following each case. Then talk about your answers with your partner or group.

Case A

Emma works in the office of a small mail-order business. Her job duties include sending out mailings and taking phone orders. Emma sends out the wrong mailer to 300 customers. Her supervisor, Antony, speaks with her. He tells her that her mistake surprised him. He says that she is usually a very careful worker. He asks her if there is anything wrong on the job or in her personal life. She becomes defensive and tells him that her personal life is her own business. Antony shrugs and says, "All right." He leaves the room. Later Emma gets a memo that says she will not be handling mailers anymore.

1. How might Emma have handled this situation in a more positive way?

   _____

   _____

2. What feedback skills did Antony show?

   _____

   _____

Case B

Ariel works as an assistant manager at a fast-food chain. She has been selected to train the new employee, Regina. While Ariel shows Regina how to operate the drink machine, Regina interrupts her. She tells Ariel that she has worked in food service before and already knows how to work the machine. Later in front of many customers, Regina handles the machine incorrectly. Soda sprays all over the counter area. After her shift, Regina leaves without a word to anyone.

1. How did Regina respond to Ariel's directions?

   _____

   _____

2. How could Regina have done things differently?

_____

_____

Case C

Belinda is a library assistant at the Homewood Valley Public
Library. She is the person who trains the library assistants. She
teaches them how to locate books on the shelves, how to check out
books for patrons, and how to use the computer. Recently she has
received a number of complaints about a new employee, Chaz.
Several library patrons have told Belinda that Chaz has been rude
to them. Belinda takes Chaz aside. "I don't want to accuse you
unfairly," she tells him. "I know you're just starting out and from
what I've seen you do a good job. But I have had a few complaints
about your attitude. I just want to make sure that there are no
major problems." To Belinda's surprise, Chaz admits that he has
been rude several times that week. "I was nervous about making
mistakes, so I snapped at a couple of people," he tells Belinda. "But
it won't happen again. I'm much more comfortable now."

What communication skills did Belinda use?

_____

_____

ACT IT OUT

Work with a partner. Imagine that you are in a fast-food restaurant.
Take turns being the restaurant worker and the restaurant
customer. The restaurant customer should give negative feedback
to the restaurant employee about the service and cleanliness of the
restaurant. As the customer gives the employee feedback, the
employee should politely respond to the criticism. When you finish,
discuss the feedback. How did each of you respond to negative
criticism?

Think and Apply

How well do you use the skills in this lesson? Complete these exercises.

A. Think about what you learned in this lesson and answer the questions. Share your answers with your partner or class.

1. Think about a time when you gave someone negative feedback. Did you give the other person information on how he or she could do things differently? Did you tell the other person anything positive? Why or why not? Would you do things differently today? How?

   _____

   _____

2. Ask a friend to teach you a new skill, such as cooking a certain dish or using a computer program. Ask for feedback as you learn. Tell your friend to include both negative and positive things. How would you rate the feedback? Did you learn anything about yourself?

   _____

   _____

B. Review your answers to A. Then answer the items.

1. Read the list of skills. Check the boxes next to your strengths.

   ☐ teaching others by giving input

   ☐ complimenting others when a task is done correctly

   ☐ listening carefully to feedback

   ☐ staying calm and avoiding anger when getting feedback

   ☐ giving negative feedback privately

2. Do you want to improve any of your skills? Which ones?

   _____

3. How do you plan to improve the skills you listed in question 2?

   _____

Performing in Today's Work Teams

What are some challenges of working on a team?

What should you contribute to your work team?

To be a team player, you must be self-motivated and accept responsibility.

You may have heard the old saying, "Two heads are better than one." It means that two or more people generally produce better results than just one person. In the workplace, employees often work in small groups, or teams. A **team** is a group of employees who work together to meet their goals.

Understand Today's Workplaces

In the past, most workers did not make decisions about their jobs. For example, a worker on an automobile assembly line was assigned one task. As long as each worker did his or her task, the job got done. The workers were not allowed to make suggestions or offer ideas.

Although employees worked together to complete tasks, they made no decisions about how they worked. They were given tasks and told how to complete them.

Today, most workers have more control over their work. Employers value the opinions and ideas of workers. A work team might make suggestions to management. For example, the team might suggest that everyone learn how to work in several different places on the assembly line. They might offer suggestions that lead to changes in the equipment or systems. Some businesses have created work teams and given those teams extra responsibilities. Work teams might be responsible for their own budgets. Teams might create their own work schedules. People who work on these teams enjoy the control over their work lives. However, work teams also have more responsibilities. To meet the extra responsibilities, each member of a team must be committed to completing tasks and being active.

Be Active

To be a "team player" you must be **self-motivated.** That means that you must be a self-starter. A self-motivated person or self-starter does not wait for someone to tell him or her what to do. Suppose you are working with a team to send five mailings out by six o'clock. At four o'clock, you notice that there is some photocopying to be done for the mailing. If you are self-motivated, you will do the photocopying yourself without being asked to do it. To be self-motivated means to think about how you can help your group.

If you think you have a good idea for your team, tell the other members. After all, terrific ideas do no good unless people hear them. Talk things out as a group. Say what you have to say and listen to what others have to say. Also try to resolve differences to reach group goals. Read the example on the next page. How does Jerry help his team?

Case Study

Rentea's Department Store had more salespeople than cash registers. Three new computer-operated registers arrived last week. But no one on staff knows how to program them and hook them up. The new registers have been in a supply closet for a week. Customers are complaining that they have to wait in long lines to pay for their purchases.

Jerry wants to help solve the problem. During his breaks, Jerry reads the manuals for the new registers. He learns how to hook them up. He calls the maintenance staff to get the extra electrical cord he will need. He decides to make some time each week to hook up one register. Two other salespeople offer to help him. After three weeks, the three registers are ready to be used. The customers can be helped with the three new registers.

Jerry is self-motivated. He does not wait for someone to tell him what needs to be done. He notices the problem. He thinks of a way that he can help. The other members of the team help to reach the team's goal.

People on work teams create schedules, assign workers to tasks, and analyze technology to meet team goals.

Decide How You Will Help Your Team

A work team can have many different responsibilities. Each person has a role. Each person works on part of a project or goal. One person might **create** schedules and **assign** workers certain job tasks. Someone else might **analyze** work technology. Analyzing technology might include figuring out what equipment will be needed and checking equipment. All team members need to communicate important information to other teams or to individuals. An example appears in the next case study.

Case Study

At Jimmy's Lobster Restaurant, employees work as a team to make customers happy. The hosts seat customers and hang up their coats. The cooks prepare meals. The waiters take orders and serve food and drinks. And the bus staff clears and resets tables. Every night before the restaurant opens, the entire staff meets for fifteen minutes. They talk about the evening ahead. The lead host starts the meeting.

Lead Host: I just looked at the reservation book and we've got four large groups coming at 7:00. And there's a group of fifteen people at 8:30.

Cook: Okay. That means we'd better get some extra salads prepared. Will you come back to the kitchen and let us know when each big party arrives?

Lead Host: Yes. The waiters and bus staff are going to have to stay on top of things, too. If the other hosts see a table that needs to be cleared, they can help the bus staff to reset it. Even if it's not their job. We need to keep things moving.

Waiters/Hosts: Okay. We will do what we can to help.

Restaurant workers meet often to discuss menus and plan for the expected number of guests.

By communicating with each other before each shift, the restaurant staff can prepare for large groups. They agree to help one another. That way, they can provide excellent service to their customers.

The restaurant work team makes their own decisions about their work. The lead host, cooks, waiters, and other hosts try to find ways to help with the amount of work. This is how many of today's work teams meet their goals. Team members speak up. They try to understand the way things work. Team members also make decisions and plan. Successful work teams enjoy the responsibility of meeting challenges.

Comprehension Check

Complete the following exercises. Refer to the lesson if necessary.

A. List three traits of today's work teams.

1. _____

2. _____

3. _____

B. What does it mean to be self-motivated?

_____

_____

C. Complete each sentence. Circle the letter in front of the answer.

1. You can help your group by

   a. leaving the important decisions for someone else.
   b. doing what you want.
   c. creating a team schedule.

2. Today's work teams

   a. make decisions.
   b. do not communicate.
   c. leave planning decisions to the management.

D. Mark the following statements T (True) or F (False).

_____ 1. A self-motivated person would <u>not</u> be a good member of a team.

_____ 2. A team is a group of employees who work together to meet their goals.

_____ 3. It is best to keep your ideas to yourself when you are working on a team.

_____ 4. Today's work teams generally have a great deal of responsibility.

Making Connections

Answer the questions following each case. Then talk about your answers with your partner or group.

Case A

At Computer Know-How, the software sales team has come up with a new approach. Each week the seven-member team has a different team leader. The team decides who will be the leader for the week. This leader comes up with ideas for better sales and service. The team leader presents his or her suggestions on Wednesday. The other members of the team respond to the team leader's suggestions. They vote on whether or not the suggestions should be carried out.

Describe how this team makes decisions.

_____

_____

_____

Case B

Danielle and Ralph work in the housekeeping department of a large hotel. Their manager meets with them to get their input on how to improve the housekeeping services. The staff plans all parts of their work. They discuss the work schedules and supplies. Danielle and Ralph decide that they will each take one of the projects.

1. Danielle studies the schedules. She notices that the staff often loses time because they arrive at a room before the hotel guest is ready to have it cleaned. Danielle suggests that the staff begin cleaning individual rooms at noon, because most people will have checked out of the hotel by then. That way, the staff can do most of the rooms at once. During the morning, the staff can clean the common areas, such as the lobby and the ballrooms. How is Danielle acting like a team member?

_____

_____

2. Ralph studies the supplies to see whether they are stored in a way that makes them easy for staff to find. While he is studying the supplies, Ralph notices that the hotel is almost out of bleach. Ralph decides not to say anything. Ordering supplies is not his job. What do you think about Ralph's decision?

_____

_____

Case C

Meridian is a floating secretary at a large law firm. Her job is to fill in for a secretary who is out sick. Meridian must also answer phones for the receptionist when the receptionist takes a break. One day, Meridian is walking to the reception desk to fill in. She notices that one of her coworkers is struggling to clear paper out of the copy machine. Meridian knows how to clear paper jams. But taking care of the copy machine is not her job.

What do you think Meridian should do?

_____

_____

_____

ACT IT OUT

Work in small groups. With your group, choose a small business that you might want to start. It can be any business you like—for example, a small restaurant, a card shop, or a car-repair business. As a group plan the creation of your product or service. Decide which tasks or duties each member of your group will be responsible for. Did each team member practice the skills from the lesson?

Think and Apply

How well do you use the skills in this lesson? Complete these exercises.

A. Think about what you learned in this lesson and answer the questions. Share your answers with your partner or your class.

1. Think of a time when you worked with a group or team to improve something. It can be something you did in a work situation or something you did at home. Were you self-motivated or did someone tell you what to do? What were your responsibilities?

   _____

   _____

2. Think about a project you would like to finish with a group at home, work, or school. Who would be included as your "staff"? What could each person do?

   _____

   _____

B. Review your answers to A. Complete the checklist. Then answer the questions that follow.

1. Read the list of skills. Check the boxes next to your strengths.
   - ☐ thinking of ways to help my group
   - ☐ performing a work task without being asked
   - ☐ communicating with my group members

2. Do you want to improve any of your skills? Which ones?

   _____

   _____

3. How do you plan to improve the skills you listed in question 2?

   _____

   _____

Communicating with Your Boss

How do you know what your boss expects from you?

How do you provide your boss with the information he or she needs?

Communicating with your boss will help you do your job well.

Imagine your communication with your boss as a flow of information back and forth. You rely on your boss for information. Your boss relies on you. To do your job well, you must find ways to keep the information flowing between you and your boss. To build a strong channel of communication with your boss, you need to speak regularly with him or her. You need to understand your job responsibilities as they change. You need to know what is expected of you. To plan and stay up-to-date about work tasks, you will probably need to speak to your boss in scheduled meetings. You may also have to provide information in quick conversations.

Understand What Your Boss Expects from You

Knowing what you should do at work sounds easy. However, sometimes you may not be sure how to proceed with a task. Suppose that you complete four reports but your boss expects five reports. In that case, there has been a failure in communication. Either you did not understand what your boss expected, or your boss did not give you the information you needed.

Start the flow of information during your interview and on your first day of work. Find out what your boss expects you to do. Learn about your job tasks. Understand your responsibilities. To keep up with changes in the company and in your job, ask your boss for regular meetings. You might have weekly or monthly meetings to stay informed. Ask your boss for his or her support with what you hope to accomplish in the company. If you know what is expected of you, you will keep up with your responsibilities. You will also keep your boss pleased with your work.

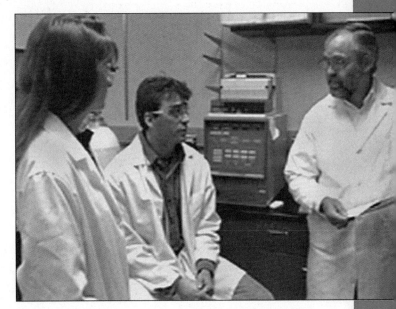

If you are asked to use technology that is new to you, ask your boss or a coworker for instruction.

Prepare Well-Written Materials

Writing memos, letters, and reports can help you to communicate information. When you prepare information for your boss, make sure that the written material is neat and easy to read. If you are writing a memo or a short report by hand, write **legibly** or clearly. Check your work. Make sure that it is complete. Fill in forms and memos completely. If you find a mistake, correct it before showing it to your boss.

If your boss asks you to prepare a long report, ask for directions. You might ask your boss for a model or sample of the writing. You can use the model as an example for you to follow. Try to make your writing similar to the model. Use the same format or design.

Speak Clearly and Concisely

Your boss may also ask you to provide oral reports. An **oral report** is spoken out loud, not written down. For example, your boss may catch you in the hall and ask you a quick question. Be prepared to answer. **Anticipate** or expect questions. Imagine what your boss might ask you. Then prepare an answer. If you keep up with your work, you will be able to answer questions easily.

When you need to ask your boss a question, try to organize your thoughts before speaking. State the purpose or reason for your question. Provide a summary. A **summary** is a list of important events or items. Then ask your question. These steps help your boss to understand what is on your mind. Here's an example.

Case Study

Bernard is a home health aide for a hospital. He visits the homes of patients who have just left the hospital. He is responsible for checking the patients. When Bernard visits Mr. Aiello, he listens to Mr. Aiello's heart and takes his temperature. Bernard writes the information on a form. When he returns to the hospital, he asks his boss a question.

Bernard: Stephanie. I have a question for you. Do you have a moment?

Stephanie: Yes.

Bernard: I visited with Mr. Aiello today. His temperature was 101 degrees. I know that the doctor asked us to watch for any changes. Should I contact the doctor?

Stephanie: Yes. The doctor should know about any changes in his condition.

Bernard: I will contact the doctor today. Thanks.

When you provide an oral report, try to speak clearly and concisely.

Bernard politely asks for Stephanie's attention. He provides a summary of his actions. This helps Stephanie begin to understand Bernard before he asks the question: "Should I contact the doctor today?" Bernard is also **concise** or brief. He only tells her the information that she needs to know. He provides a short oral report. Because Bernard presented the information clearly, Stephanie can respond. Consider a different way that Bernard might speak to Stephanie.

Case Study

Bernard: Stephanie, do you have a minute?

Stephanie: Yes.

Bernard: Today, I drove over to Mr. Aiello's house. The traffic was terrible. Anyway, I asked him how he was feeling and he said fine. And then I took his temperature and checked his heart. And I talked to him for a little while. He said he would expect to see me in a couple of days. I said OK. But what I wanted to ask you is this: If Mr. Aiello's temperature is high, should I contact the doctor in a couple of days? I thought I remembered that you said something about that. What do you think?

If you were Stephanie, you might become impatient with Bernard. It is hard to understand the reason for Bernard's question. He gives other information that is confusing. By speaking about the traffic, he is not staying on point. He is not concise. He is not giving Stephanie the information she needs to answer his question. Bernard is not communicating well. He is making it hard for his boss to understand what he is asking her.

Organize your thoughts before you speak to your boss. When you are ready to speak, remember to be confident and clear. Remember to use the skills in the lesson to keep the communication flowing.

Comprehension Check

Complete the following exercises. Refer to the lesson if necessary.

A. List three traits of well-written materials.

1. _____

2. _____

3. _____

B. List three things you should do when speaking to your boss.

1. _____

2. _____

3. _____

C. Complete each sentence. Circle the letter in front of the answer.

1. Communicating with your boss means sharing information
   a. by speaking.
   b. by writing.
   c. by speaking and writing.

2. If you write a memo that is not legible, your boss
   a. will not be able to read it.
   b. will think that you are confident.
   c. will become defensive.

3. Before asking your boss a question, you should try to
   a. organize your thoughts before speaking.
   b. understand what is on your boss's mind.
   c. prepare a long report.

D. Mark the following statements T (True) or F (False).

_____ 1. Memos, letters, and reports are forms of written communication.

_____ 2. Being concise means being brief.

_____ 3. An oral report is a written report.

Answer the questions following each case. Then talk about your answers with your partner or group.

Case A

Sharon is an operating engineer. She operates a crane at a construction site. Sharon is on her way to her crane one morning when her supervisor, Dale, asks quickly about a safety report. He says: "Sharon, when do you think you will turn in your safety report?" Sharon says: "You never told me about a report."

1. How does Sharon respond?

_____

_____

2. If Dale did tell Sharon about the report, but she forgot about it, how should she try to improve?

_____

_____

Case B

Alex is a catering assistant in a hotel. He helps to make arrangements for catered events such as weddings and business meetings. Customers call Alex to learn about the menus, prices, and sizes of the event rooms. The catering manager, Nancy, asks Alex to review the catered events files for the past six months. She asks Alex to prepare a report summarizing the most popular menu items at those events. She tells Alex where to find the files. Alex is worried about this assignment because he has not prepared this type of report before.

What should Alex do?

_____

_____

_____

Case C

Ann and Franklin are salespeople for the Ginger Tea Company. They are having a monthly sales meeting with Kimberlee Shapiro, the manager. Ann and Franklin are meeting with Kimberlee to discuss how many sales calls they have made. Ann tells Kimberlee about the number of calls and sales she has made. She says she feels good about her work. She hopes to finish her calls this week. Franklin tells a long story about an unpleasant customer. He talks about the different brands of teas and why people do not want to buy them. He looks through his notes to find out how many calls he has made.

1. Describe Ann's oral report. How is she providing information for her boss?

    _____

    _____

2. Do you think Franklin is providing helpful information for this meeting? Why or why not?

    _____

    _____

    _____

TALK IT OUT

Work with a partner. Take turns practicing your ability to provide brief oral summaries. You will need a newspaper. Select an article from the newspaper and read it. Make notes of important facts. Note the order of events in the article. Then provide a concise summary for your partner. Your partner can ask questions, if necessary. Your partner should repeat what you have reported. Then switch roles and repeat the activity with a new article.

Think and Apply

How well do you use the skills in this lesson? Complete these exercises.

A. Think about what you learned in this lesson and answer the questions. Share your answers with your partner or your class.

1. Choose a piece of writing that you want to give to someone else. The writing can be a letter to a friend, a report for your boss, or a shopping list. How can you provide well-written material?

   _____

   _____

2. Think about a conversation you have had with a boss or teacher. Did you provide information that was useful? Were you confident and concise?

   _____

   _____

B. Review your answers to A. Complete the checklist. Then answer the questions that follow.

1. Read the list of skills. Check the boxes next to your strengths.

   ☐ understanding what my boss expects from me

   ☐ providing brief and concise oral reports

   ☐ providing summaries

   ☐ using legible handwriting

2. Do you want to improve any of your skills? Which ones?

   _____

   _____

3. How do you plan to improve the skills you listed in question 2?

   _____

   _____

Practicing Effective Telephone Communication

What can you do to prepare for a phone call?

What should you do if you cannot answer a caller's question?

How do you like to be treated when you are on the phone?

To be successful in the workplace, you must learn to communicate effectively on the phone.

Most businesses could not operate without a telephone. Customers use the phone to order merchandise, to ask questions, and sometimes to complain. Employees use the phone to call in if they are going to be late. Employers need to know that you will make a good impression when you talk to people on the telephone.

Be Prepared

Before you answer the phone, make sure that you have a message pad and several pens or pencils. Ask your coworkers what questions people ask when they call. Find out the answers to these questions. You may need the following information:

- the phone numbers of other employees so that you can transfer a call

- directions telling you how to transfer a call on your phone

- the address of your workplace

- the fax number for your workplace, if there is one

- how to put a caller on hold

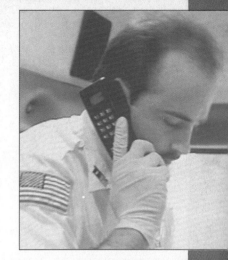

Clear and effective telephone communication between hospitals and paramedics is critical during emergency situations.

These are basic functions of the phone system. If you do not know these functions, you might find yourself in a situation that you cannot correct. Imagine that a client calls for a coworker. Instead of putting that person on hold you cut that person off the line. Clearly this mistake is not good for business. Know how to use the phone to maintain good relationships with clients and customers.

Follow Procedures for Answering a Call

Do you know what to say when you answer the phone? Follow these guidelines.

- Identify yourself. State your workplace and your name. Say something like, "Apple Appliances, Sam speaking."

- Speak clearly and slowly, because the caller cannot see you.

- Be polite. You are trying to make a good impression on the caller.

- Give the caller your full attention. Stop what you are doing before you answer the phone. Don't work and talk on the phone at the same time.

- Listen carefully to what the caller says.

- Take notes on your message pad. Write the caller's name and why he or she is calling.

- Ask questions if you aren't sure what the caller wants.

- Summarize what the caller has said at the end of your call. You can use your notes.

At first, you may choose to keep a list of these steps by your phone as a guide. After about a week, you will have developed a routine for answering the phone. Read the case study to see how Elsie uses her phone skills.

Case Study

The phone rings at the courthouse where Elsie works. Elsie identifies herself. She says, "Main County Courthouse. Elsie speaking."

"Hi. My name is Tamisha Jackson. Can you give me directions to the courthouse?" While Tamisha speaks, Elsie listens carefully and takes notes. She writes down the words, "Tamisha Jackson" and "directions."

"Yes, Ms. Jackson. Will you be coming from the south?" By using the caller's name and asking a question, Elsie shows that she is listening.

It is acceptable to put a caller on hold if you return to the caller in a timely way.

Some callers may ask questions that you do not know the answer to. In that case, you have three choices. You can put the caller on hold while you find out the answer to the question. Say, "I will look that up for you. Just a moment." Or, you may transfer the call to a coworker who knows the answer. Say something like, "I am going to transfer you to the Accounting Department. They can answer that question for you." If you need to take extra time to find an answer, tell the caller that is what you will do. Take down the caller's name and number. Then get the answer and call the person back. Your caller will like the fact that you did not leave him or her on hold for a long time.

Make a Call

Making a call is not very different from answering a call. First, write down the reason you are calling and any questions you may need to ask. Then make the call. When someone answers, identify yourself. State your name and the reason you are calling. Say something like, "Hello. This is Jerome Norback. I would like to make an appointment with Dr. Hansen." During the conversation, speak slowly and clearly. Listen carefully to the person you are talking to. Take notes if you need to. Be polite. If you don't understand something, ask questions.

Satisfy Your Caller

You may get calls from people who are angry. Even if a caller is rude, you must be polite. Your goal is to change the caller's bad impression into a good impression. Follow these guidelines.

- Listen carefully to the caller's complaint. Do not interrupt the caller.

- Summarize the caller's complaint. Show the caller that you understand his or her point of view. Say something like, "I am glad you called. That is a serious problem."

- Suggest a solution. If a caller is angry about defective merchandise, you might say, "Would you like us to replace that for you?" You may not be able to think of a solution. In that case, tell the caller that you don't know how to solve the problem, but that you will find out. Then ask the caller to wait for a moment while you ask your supervisor what to do.

- Tell the caller what action you or your employer will take in response to the complaint.

- Apologize even if it was not your fault.

Like the first phone list, you may choose to keep a list of these steps near your phone.

Communicating on the phone can be harder than communicating face-to-face. People talking on the phone sometimes misunderstand each other. To avoid misunderstandings, be extra polite and listen extra carefully. Good telephone skills will make you a valuable employee.

Comprehension Check

Complete the following exercises. Refer to the lesson if necessary.

A. Name three ways that you can prepare to answer the phone.

1. _____

2. _____

3. _____

B. Complete each sentence. Circle the letter in front of the answer.

1. The *first* thing you should do when you answer the phone or make a call is

   a. summarize what the caller said.
   b. identify yourself.
   c. apologize to the caller.

2. Because your caller cannot see you, you need to

   a. speak slowly and clearly.
   b. ask a question.
   c. take notes.

3. To change a caller's bad impression into a good impression, you should

   a. show the caller that you understand his or her point of view.
   b. tell the caller to call back later and ask for your supervisor.
   c. not apologize unless it is your fault.

4. If you do not know the answer to a caller's question, you should

   a. transfer the call to a coworker who knows the answer.
   b. make up an answer to please the caller.
   c. apologize and politely hang up.

C. Mark the following statements T (True) or F (False).

_____ 1. When a customer calls with a complaint, you should interrupt the customer in order to apologize.

_____ 2. While a caller is speaking, you should listen and take notes.

Making Connections

Answer the questions following each case. Then talk about your answers with your partner or group.

Case A

Myra works for a temporary agency. One morning, Myra arrives at work. She will be filling in for a receptionist who is out sick. The phone rings and Myra answers, "CBC Construction, Myra speaking."

The caller says, "This is Gladys Sykes. Please tell Karl Withers that I will not be able to speak to him at eleven o'clock. He can call me at two. My number is 555-7328." Gladys thinks she can remember the message and the number. She decides to just write it down later. She says, "Thank you, I'll tell him."

Myra hangs up the phone. She chants the phone number to herself. "5-5-5, 7-3-2-8. 5-5-5, 7-3-2-8." Finally, she finds a crumpled up envelope in the garbage. She writes the phone number. By this time, Myra does not remember anything but the phone number. She does not even know who called.

How could preparing to answer the phone have helped Myra?

_____

_____

Case B

Louis works for a social service agency. The agency provides legal help to people who cannot afford a lawyer. One afternoon, the phone rings while Louis is busy filing papers. The caller says, "My sister needs a lawyer. Her friend fell and sprained his ankle in Rose's apartment. Now he is suing her!" While the caller speaks, Louis continues to put papers into the file cabinet. Louis says, "Wait a minute. You want to sue your sister? Because you fell down? I don't understand."

What telephone skills could Louis have used to help him understand the caller?

_____

Case C

Duane is the customer service representative for an electronics store. One morning, a customer calls to complain about a TV that doesn't work. The caller yells at Duane and is rude. Duane listens carefully to the caller and takes notes. When the caller stops talking, Duane says, "Let me see if I understand you correctly. When you turn on your TV, all you see is a line across the screen. That is a serious problem. However, our staff should be able to repair the TV for you. I am sorry this caused you so much inconvenience. Let me know if you have other problems."

Do you think Duane provides good customer service? Why or why not? List at least two examples from the case to support your answer.

_____

_____

_____

TRY IT OUT

Work with a small group. You will need a newspaper. You may also need a phone book. Look through the newspaper. Find an advertisement for a community meeting, a festival, or another event that you would like to attend. (Do not choose a movie, because movie information is provided by a recording. Choose an event where you will have to get information from a live person.) With your group, prepare to phone for information. List the information you want to know about the event. Write down the questions you will need to ask. One person from your group should make the phone call. The person who makes the phone call should tell the group how he or she prepared for the call, the questions he or she asked, and what he or she learned. Each group should report its results to the class.

Think and Apply

How well do you use the skills in this lesson? Complete these exercises.

A. Think about what you learned in this lesson and answer the questions. Share your answers with your partner or your class.

1. Remember the last time that you spoke to someone on the phone. What phone skills did you use? Are there any phone skills that you wish you had used?

   _____

   _____

2. Practice your telephone skills at home. Think of some information that you need to know. Maybe you are looking for an apartment or a new television. Call someone on the phone to get more information. For example, if you are looking for an apartment, phone a building manager. Ask questions about apartments that are available. What phone skills did you use?

   _____

   _____

B. Review your answers to A. Complete the checklist. Then answer the questions that follow.

1. Read the list of skills. Check the boxes next to your strengths.

   ☐ preparing for a call   ☐ listening

   ☐ identifying myself   ☐ taking notes

   ☐ speaking clearly and slowly   ☐ asking questions

   ☐ being polite   ☐ summarizing

   ☐ giving the caller my complete attention   ☐ suggesting solutions to problems

2. Do you want to improve any of your skills? Which ones?

   _____

3. How do you plan to improve the skills you listed in question 2?

   _____

Check What You've Learned

Check What You've Learned will give you an idea of how well you've learned communication skills you'll need to use in the workplace.

Read each question. Circle the letter before the answer.

1. Andrew Johnson is an inventory clerk at a warehouse. Andrew should answer his phone by saying

   a. "Warehouse."
   b. "City Wholesale Supply. This is Andrew Johnson."
   c. "Yeah?"

2. Joan is attending a sales department meeting at her company. They are discussing new products. Joan has a lot of ideas on how to advertise the new products. Joan should

   a. criticize everyone's ideas except her own.
   b. explain her ideas, listen to everyone else's ideas, and then help the group decide which ideas to use.
   c. keep quiet and after the meeting send the head of the department a memo that explains her ideas.

3. LaWanda repairs photocopy machines. Every day she drives to different offices in the city. Each Friday she meets with her boss to talk about her week. During the meetings, LaWanda should

   a. interrupt her report several times to complain about traffic and weather that week.
   b. focus her report on which companies' machines needed repairing that week and how she fixed them.
   c. discuss why she thinks her customers need to buy newer copiers that won't break down so often.

4. Sally is a teller at City National Bank. One day she sees that the teller next to her is having trouble communicating with a customer, who speaks only Spanish. Sally knows some Spanish. She should

   a. use her Spanish to translate for the customer.
   b. stay focused on her own work.
   c. wait until her break and then tell the other teller that she should learn some Spanish, too.

5. A technician is showing Andre how to use his new computer. The technician speaks quickly and uses words that Andre doesn't know. Andre should

   a. pretend that he understands and, after the technician has left, ask a coworker to help him.
   b. ask to be transferred to a department that does not use computers.
   c. ask the technician to speak more slowly so that Andre can take notes and ask questions.

6. Eduardo is in charge of his company's mail room. One of the employees, Ben, takes a long time to deliver the mail. Sometimes Ben gives mail to the wrong people. Eduardo should

   a. not say anything to Ben and hope that his work improves.
   b. ask Ben to work faster and more carefully.
   c. tell Ben that he will be fired if he doesn't improve.

7. Monique is explaining a task to another employee, Kip. Kip's hearing is not very good, and his work area is noisy. Monique should

   a. move to a quieter area and explain the task to Kip slowly.
   b. assign Kip to a lower paying job in a quieter area of the warehouse.
   c. explain the task in as few words as possible.

8. Carmen, Gerard, and Harriet assemble car stereos. They have trouble completing their work because the stereo parts are kept far from their work area. Their work area does not have room for both the finished stereos and the boxes of parts. So they have to stop working each time they need more parts. They should

   a. ask the factory manager to reduce the number of stereos they have to assemble each day.
   b. grumble to each other and their coworkers about the problem.
   c. brainstorm together until they come up with a solution.

9. Rosa is applying for the job of host at a restaurant. She feels nervous because she does not like job interviews. Rosa should

    a. avoid looking at the interviewer because that will make her more nervous.

    b. try to smile, maintain eye contact, and sit up straight as she talks to the interviewer.

    c. explain to the interviewer that she does not like job interviews but will be fine when talking to customers.

10. Tanya is a human relations specialist. She is talking with Mr. Rodriguez, who needs a new executive assistant. He has many requirements for the position and has been talking for a long time. Tanya should

    a. tell him the kind of employee she thinks he needs.

    b. nod her head, look at Mr. Rodriguez, and say, "Go on" or "OK," once in a while as she takes notes.

    c. listen silently and keep her eyes focused on her notebook as she takes notes.

Review Chart

This chart shows you what lessons you should review. Reread each question you missed. Then look at the appropriate lesson of the book for help in understanding the correct answer.

Question Check the questions you missed.	Skill The exercise, like the book, focuses on the skills below.	Lesson Review what you learned in this book.
1. _____	Handling business calls	10
2. _____	Working with others	5
3. _____	Communicating with your boss	9
4. _____	Being a team player	8
5. _____	Getting information	2
6. _____	Giving helpful feedback	7
7. _____	Giving directions	3
8. _____	Reaching a compromise	6
9. _____	Giving a positive message	4
10. _____	Listening	1

Glossary

aggressive (work style) A forceful way of working, such as taking charge of a group and trying to make decisions for others. page 37

analyze To study a problem by carefully examining its parts. page 62

anticipate To look ahead to things that may happen. page 70

assertive (work style) A way of working in which a person is confident about offering ideas or opinions, and pays attention to others' ideas. page 37

assign To give out a task or to select someone to do a task. page 62

brainstorming A way for a person or a group to find a solution to a problem by listing all the ideas they can think of. page 46

clarify To make clear or easy to understand. page 15

communication barriers Things that block the flow of information, such as using confusing language. page 14

compromise A way of settling disagreements in which each person agrees to give up part of what he or she wants. page 45

concise Brief; short; to the point. page 71

create To make or produce. page 62

creative problem-solving The ability to solve problems in new or unexpected ways. page 46

interpret To present an explanation of something to oneself or others. page 22

interpersonal skills Abilities to relate and work with other people, such as listening carefully, speaking politely, and being friendly. page 38

jargon Technical words and phrases that workers in a particular job understand but other people may not. page 14

legibly Easy to read. page 69

model To demonstrate a process or a task. page 53

negative feedback Criticism given to someone about his or her work or actions. page 52

negotiation A way of reaching an agreement in which each person or side discusses possible solutions. page 44

nonverbal cues (also nonverbal messages) Body language that indicates one's feelings, such as nodding, smiling, or frowning. pages 6, 30

oral report A spoken presentation. page 70

paraphrasing Putting into your own words information that you have read or heard. page 22

passive (work style) A way of working in which a person stays in the background and lets other people make decisions. page 37

point of view   The way a person looks at something. pages 21, 39, 44

positive feedback   Praise given to someone about his or her work or actions. page 52

self-motivated   Able to recognize that a task needs to be done and to do it without being told. page 61

slang   Informal language. page 14

summarize   To give a short version of information including only the most important points. page 7

summary   A shortened version of information including only the most important points. page 70

team   A group of employees who work together to accomplish a goal. page 60

verbal cues   Short comments from a listener that indicate such things as attention, understanding, or confusion. page 5

visual aids   Objects or drawings that help to show what you mean, such as maps, charts, and diagrams. page 21

vocabulary   Words that a person uses. page 28

Answer Key

For many exercises in this book, several answers are possible. You may want to share your answers with your teacher or another learner.

Check What You Know (page 1)
1. (a)   2. (b)   3. (b)   4. (c)
5. (a)   6. (a)   7. (b)   8. (c)
9. (a)   10. (c)

Lesson 1

Comprehension Check (page 8)
A. Answers include: "Yes," "I see," and "go on."
B. Answers include: nodding, leaning forward, smiling.
C. 1. (b)   2. (a)   3. (a)   4. (a)

Making Connections (page 9)
Case A
> Answers include: focusing, asking questions to understand the message, summarizing.

Case B
> Answers include: Mark looked puzzled because Jan did not listen to any part of what he said. Her response did not make sense. Jan caused the confusion by interrupting Mark. She did not allow him to finish his thought, and she responded inappropriately.

Case C
> asking questions

Case D
> 1. No. Answers include: Jennifer is too busy looking for something. She is not facing him.
> 2. Answers include: Jennifer turns her back toward Carter. This nonverbal cue tells Carter that she is not listening. He starts to speak and then stops.

Lesson 2

Comprehension Check (page 16)
A. Answers include: identify specific points you don't understand, ask for clarification or repetition, ask about words you don't understand.
B. Answers include avoiding problems, solving problems, clearing up confusion, gaining important information.
C. Answers include: talking too fast, using slang, using jargon, being vague, not giving complete directions.
D. 1. T   2. T   3. F   4. F
   5. F   6. T   7. T   8. F

Making Connections (page 17)
Case A
> Answers include the following: What questions do you ask? How do you complete the calls so quickly?

Case B
> Answers include the following: When is the move? What should we do to prepare? Will we receive private offices?

Case C
> 1. Answers include: bores, blueprints, feed and speeds, CAD/CAM. The language is called jargon.
> 2. Possible questions include: "What are bores? What are blueprints? What do *feed* and *speeds* mean? What is a CAD/CAM?"

Lesson 3

Comprehension Check (page 24)
A. Answers include: maps, charts, blueprints, simple drawings, and diagrams.
B. interpret and paraphrase
C. 1. point of view
   2. paraphrasing
   3. visual aid
D. 1. F   2. T   3. F   4. T

Making Connections (page 25)

Case A
1. Answers include: She could have repeated or paraphrased the information; she could have asked questions about unclear information; she could have taken notes.
2. He could use visual aids, such as an example of the notice.

Case B
1. visual aid
2. Answers include: to save time; to make sure the forms were done correctly; to answer questions Ms. Contreras might have.

Case C
   He'll organize and mail ten brochures Tuesday; he'll describe a video to Mary today and ask for the title. Then he'll call a woman in Florida to tell her the title and mail her a brochure Thursday.

Lesson 4

Comprehension Check (page 32)

A. 1. F   2. T   3. F   4. F
B. 1. (a)   2. (c)   3. (b)   4. (b)

Making Connections (page 33)

Case A
   Answers include: Batina started the conversation by saying that she wanted to help, but then she didn't pay much attention to Seth. Her words didn't match her body language. Batina should have looked Seth in the eye and paid attention.

Case B
   Answers include: Wanda's body language tells Sean that she does not care about what he thinks. When Wanda works with a client, she should talk proudly, listen, and look the client directly in the eye. If she's never met the client, she should introduce herself.

Case C
   Molly provides a mixed message. She praises Gail, but also gives her a new task. Molly also does not explain the new task. Her directions are unclear.

Lesson 5

Comprehension Check (page 40)

A. aggressive, assertive, passive
B. Answers include: listening carefully, being friendly, and speaking politely.
C. 1. (c)   2. (a)

Making Connections (page 41)

Case A
1. Marisa-aggressive; Lukas and Alice-passive
2. Answers include the following: Everyone in a group must contribute. Marisa should let others speak. Alice and Lukas should offer their ideas.

Case B
   Answers include: Theo should be more patient with a new employee who may be nervous about speaking up in a meeting. Theo could improve these skills: being polite and considering Rafael's point of view.

Case C
1. Answers include that they are each describing the accident from their own point of view.
2. Yes. Answers include that a van was in the way so they could not see the other car.

Lesson 6

Comprehension Check (page 48)

A. Answers include: each group member should contribute; everyone needs to accept new ideas; group members must set goals.
B. 1. T   2. T
C. 1. (b)   2. (a)   3. (a)   4. (c)

Making Connections (page 49)

Case A
1. Answers include: An end-of-the-week bonus for the employee who sells the most pairs of shoes (no matter what the price); a monthly award for the employee who shows the most courtesy to customers.

2. Answers include that the manager wanted to involve all the salespeople in solving the problem.

Case B

They used brainstorming when they each made suggestions, and they let Avia's suggestion lead them to Allen's suggestion.

Lesson 7

Comprehension Check (page 56)

A. Answers include: compliment others on what they do well; avoid getting angry; model the skill or process and have others imitate you.

B. Answers include: a compliment; a good performance evaluation.

C. Answers include: allow yourself time to correct your performance; make a plan for improving; get advice from coworkers.

D. Answers include: it is hard to listen to feedback when someone is angry with you; it is hard to give useful feedback when you are angry; getting angry makes it hard for people to work together as a team.

E. 1. (b)   2. (c)

Making Connections (page 57)

Case A

1. Answers include: Emma should have held her temper. She might have told Antony the possible causes of her mistake. She might have apologized for her mistake.
2. Answers include: He complimented Emma on her work record; he offered her a chance to confide in him or explain her mistake; he did not get angry when Emma became defensive; he took steps so that the mistake wouldn't happen again.

Case B

1. Answers include: She cut Ariel off; she pretended to know something she didn't; she made a mess in front of customers; she didn't apologize afterward.
2. Answers include: She could have listened to Ariel even though she thought she knew how to run the machine; she could have apologized to Ariel and her coworkers afterward.

Case C

Answers include that she listens to Chaz. She tells him some good things about his job performance. She makes him feel comfortable with the feedback.

Lesson 8

Comprehension Check (page 64)

A. Answers include: They have more control; they provide input; they do more than one task or have many responsibilities.

B. Answers include: to act on one's own; to think of ways to help the group; to be a self-starter.

C. 1. (c)   2. (a)

D. 1. F   2. T   3. F   4. T

Making Connections (page 65)

Case A

Answers include: the team works together; each member provides input.

Case B

1. Answers include: She is taking responsibility for group goals. She makes a suggestion for improvement.
2. Answers include: Ralph is not acting like a team member. He should take responsibility for work that needs to be done, especially because a supply shortage will affect everyone.

Case C

Answers should include that Meridian should stop and help to clear the paper jam, even though it is not part of her job.

Lesson 9

Comprehension Check (page 72)

A. Answers include: neat, easy to read, complete, legible.

B. Answers include: be clear, confident, and concise; provide a summary; anticipate questions.

C. 1. (c)   2. (a)   3. (a)

D. 1. T   2. T   3. F

Making Connections (page 73)

Case A

1. Sharon responds defensively.
2. Answers include that Sharon should take the feedback and try to remember deadlines.

Case B

Answers include: Alex could ask Nancy for further directions such as if there is a model or sample report he could use as an example; he could summarize the steps of the assignment for Nancy and ask if he is forgetting anything.

Case C

1. Answers include that she has provided a summary of her sales calls; she is brief and concise; she also appears confident.
2. No. Answers include: Franklin is talking about things other than the number of sales calls; he is also unprepared and unorganized; he looks through his notes to find the information he needs for the meeting; he is not concise; he does not provide a helpful summary.

Lesson 10

Comprehension Check (page 80)

A. Answers include making sure that you have a message pad and pens or pencils, asking your coworkers what questions people usually ask when they call and gathering information such as the address of your workplace, the fax number, and information you need to transfer a call.

B. 1. (b)   2. (a)   3. (a)   4. (a)

C. 1. F   2. T

Making Connections (page 81)

Case A

Answers include that if Myra had prepared by making sure she had a note pad and several pens and pencils ready, she could have taken notes.

Case B

Answers include that Louis does use some telephone skills: He asks questions to help him understand. However, Louis should have stopped working to listen to the caller. He also should have taken notes while the caller was talking.

Case C

Answers include: Yes, Duane provides good customer service. Examples include: listening carefully, not interrupting, summarizing the caller's complaint, understanding the caller's point of view, suggesting a solution, apologizing for the problem.

Check What You've Learned (page 84)

1. (b)   2. (b)   3. (b)   4. (a)

5. (c)   6. (b)   7. (a)   8. (c)

9. (b)   10. (b)